VISIONS OF THE NETHERLANDS

Frans Lemmens

Text
Martijn de Rooi

dutch publishers

Visions of the Netherlands
A Dutch Publishers publication
Publishers
Allard de Rooi, Wilbert Collet
Production
The Ad Agency, Alphen aan den Rijn
Concept and design
Allard de Rooi
Cover design
Maarten van der Kroft
Photography
Frans Lemmens (except page 79)
Text
Martijn de Rooi
Translation
Tony Burrett
DTP and production
Maurits Eykman
Lithography
Studio Telstar, Pijnacker
Printing
Scholma Druk, Bedum
With thanks to
Marjolijn van Steeden, Wendy Collet,
Siebe Meijer, Sylvia Pessireron

Final processing photographic material:
FE NOB-FOTO BV. Telephone (035) 677 8043.

ISBN 90-76214-02-6 (English)
ISBN 90-76214-03-4 (Dutch)

Trade distribution
Nilsson & Lamm BV, P.O. Box 195, 1380 AD
Weesp, the Netherlands. Telephone (0294)
49 49 49. Fax (0294) 49 44 55. E-mail:
info@nilsson-lamm.nl.

Dutch Publishers and Dutchshop are trade
names of The Ad Agency, P.O. Box 340,
2400 AH Alphen aan den Rijn,
The Netherlands.
Tel. (0172) 449 333. Fax (0172) 495 846.
E-mail: info@theadagency.nl

Sixth printing: March 2006

Captions page 4-9
Page 4-5: **The picturesque canals of
Amsterdam.** Page 6-7: **Tulips in the rain.**
Page 8-9: **Windmills at Kinderdijk in the
province of South Holland.**

Water 10

Landscape 32

The Structures 52

Visions of the Netherlands

S even million tourists and vast numbers of business people visit the Netherlands each year – and many Netherlanders live and work in other countries. These people all have one thing in common – they cherish their own images, their own visions, of this little country by the North Sea. And they share these visions and images, each in their own way, with their friends, their families and their business colleagues, so even those who have never visited the Netherlands have their own vision of it.

The 250 photos in 'Visions of the Netherlands' give a modern and realistic image of the country. They show the Netherlands as it is now, and how people see it every day. This book does not confine itself to the capital, Amsterdam, so popular with visitors, but also shows dozens of less visited places, some of which, had they been situated elsewhere, might well have become world famous. It shows the Netherlander in his everyday environment, at work, at play or in his favourite pub.

No one book can pretend to offer a complete picture of a country. This one certainly does not. What it does try to do is to give a broad impression of the Netherlands' many facets, as seen through the eyes of one of her best photographers, a craftsman whose favourite subject is the land he lives in.

The Netherlands is a hospitable country and easy to travel round. We hope that this book will inspire many – both Netherlanders and visitors – to learn more of it and, in the learning, create their very own visions of the Netherlands.

Water

No country in the world is more strongly associated with water than the Netherlands. 'The Dutch stand in it and it pours down on their heads' - a comment as pointed as it is humorous. Not an enviable place to live in, these wetlands, one might think. But nobody understands the art of taming water better than the Netherlander. He barricaded his coasts with dams and dikes and created a refuge where life was no longer dictated by the rhythm of the tides.

The Low Countries

Much of the Netherlands is a delta formed by three big rivers – the Rhine, the Maas and the Schelde – and from ancient times ingenious solutions have had to be found to help the people keep their heads above water. Almost a quarter of the country lies below sea level and without adequate safeguards it would disappear beneath the waves. The lowest point (6.74 metres below sea level) is in Nieuwerkerk aan den IJssel - this was officially established when both Nieuwerkerk and a rival municipality claimed the title of the 'Lowest Point of the Netherlands'. In a country whose name translates appropriately as the 'Low Countries', this title is a source of pride.

The low-lying position of the Netherlands intrigues and fascinates many foreigners. Land below sea level, what does that look like? Many imagine the Low Countries as marshy, half-submerged pastureland. A surprise awaits them at Schiphol, the national airport, because although it lies 4.5 metres below sea level – there is a yardstick to prove it – Schiphol is actually as dry as a bone. Only its name is a reminder of the days when there was a notorious bay here, a graveyard ('scheepshol') for sailing ships.

Page 10-11
**Three swans on the frozen Loosdrechtse Plassen – preparing for a rehearsal of the famous ballet Swan Lake, perhaps? The seven 'plassen' (lakes), in the province of Utrecht, are an important nature reserve and recreation area. They were created between the 13th and 19th centuries when layers of peat were 'cut' from peat bogs. When dried, this was used as fuel. The lakes are not only a popular attraction for a variety of feathered visitors, but also for watersports and skating enthusiasts.
The boat in the small photograph, taken near Sandfirden in the province of Friesland, is a 'Lemsteraak'.**

Above and below
Along the Dutch coast lighthouses, such as this one at Nieuw-Haamstede in the province of Zeeland, show ships the way (above). **The facades of merchants' houses, reflected in Brouwersgracht in Amsterdam** (below).

Champions at controlling water

Huge water works were necessary to make the Netherlands dry and habitable, and the Netherlander was forced to become a specialist in hydraulic engineering. Nowadays, he is regarded internationally as the champion in water control and he leads the field when there is something to salvage, dredge or build in foreign waters. Impoldering, land reclamation, constructing bridges and harbours, the Netherlander can compete with the best. This sterling reputation is partly due to Hans Brinker, the young literary hero of American origin, who made history by sticking his finger in a hole in the dike, preventing catastrophic flooding.

The struggle against the water has been going on for centuries but in modern times one event in particular greatly influenced its course. In 1953, the south-west provinces of the country were ravaged by a freak flood tide driven by gale force winds and 1835 people lost their lives. Again the traditional enemy had demonstrated just how vulnerable the Netherlands is, and to prevent a repetition the Netherlander was once more forced to call upon his engineering genius. He struck back with the Delta Plan, a massive complex of water control mechanisms designed to guarantee safety for the South Holland and Zeeland islands and which, at the same time, reduced the length of the North Sea coast from 1080 to about 380 kilometres. The jewel in the crown of the Delta Works is the flood barrier in the Nieuwe Waterweg, a later addition completed in 1997, which is a hydraulic engineering masterpiece of the first order.

But water is still omnipresent in the Netherlands. It is hard to find a place which does not have a view of a lake, pool, river, canal, waterway, ditch, stream or small harbour. Waterways have always been widely used for transport, in the countryside even cattle are carried by boat. Moreover, water fulfils a recreational role – in winter, too, when the Dutch en masse surrender to what is almost a sacred national custom – skating. There is good reason why a swimming diploma is the first in a long series of certificates that every Netherlander is expected to obtain during the course of his lifetime.

Terps and polders

The struggle against the watery enemy was originally fought with modest means. Between 500 BC and 650 AD the people of Friesland erected around a thousand artificial refuges, up to fifteen metres in height, called 'terps' (mounds), on which they built houses and villages. The sea level continued to rise and heightening these mounds was a recurring ritual. To some extent this occurred naturally as rubbish and manure accumulated.

Under pressure from the rising waters, the settling of the soil, the increasing population and countless catastrophes, both large and small – and with many ups and downs – the Netherlander mastered the art of controlling the waters. From

Left
Characteristic river views in the province of Gelderland: the IJssel at Terwolde (above) **and cargo vessels on the Waal at Ochten** (below).

Above and below
A wanderer, lost in thought, on a stormy North Sea beach near Camperduin in the province of North Holland (above) **and a party of 'wadlopers' (mud flat walkers) off the island of Ameland** (below) **illustrate the important recreational function of the water.**

Above, below and right
Water is also an excellent highway when it is frozen, at least for those who know how to adapt to the situation! Locomotion on ice is difficult; it requires practice and the proper equipment. A pair of spiked clogs suffices (above), **but those who prefer to 'get a move on' may find a bicycle** (below) **or - much safer - a pair of skates more useful. Many Netherlanders learn to skate before they learn to ride a bicycle, so it is not surprising that the country has produced so many champion speed skaters! The ice skating marathon the 'Elfstedentocht', held only in the very coldest winters, is a unique event** (see pages 102-103). **A loving mother on the frozen IJsselmeer near the lighthouse at Marken demonstrates how the tradition is passed on** (right).

14

1000 AD onwards dikes were constructed and this created the opportunity to drain stretches of land, but the technology to carry out large-scale projects was still lacking. This came in the 14th century, in the form of the windmill, something which today is still a characteristic feature of the Dutch landscape. The perfected windmills, connected in series, were able to pump large lakes dry. The hydraulic engineer and windmill builder with the rather apt name of Leeghwater ('Empty water') was very much the vogue in the 17th century as, with the aid of dozens of windmills, he transformed one lake after another into a polder.

The most spectacular reclamations, however, the Haarlemmermeer and IJsselmeer polders, date from after the introduction of the steam-driven, and later the electric-powered, pumping station. The IJsselmeer project was the work of the hydraulic engineer Cornelis Lely, the brain behind enclosing the Zuider Zee. Soon after the province of North Holland had been ravaged by heavy flooding, he was given the green light for the construction of the thirty-kilometre-long Afsluitdijk, which was completed in 1932. The Zuider Zee – a huge bay cut by the sea – became an inland lake, the IJsselmeer, which was then partially reclaimed. Lely's services were so highly regarded that Lelystad, a city in one of the new polders, was named after him.

How much the modern Netherlander owes to men like Leeghwater and Lely is demonstrated by the fact that about twenty percent of the country's land area has been reclaimed from the waters. Their achievements are summed up briefly but eloquently in the saying 'God created the world, but the Netherlanders created the Netherlands.'

An indissoluble bond

But water is not only the Netherlands' enemy. It also has its useful and pleasant aspects – for example, you can sail on it – and the Netherlander has always exploited this very well. Throughout the centuries he played a leading role in shipping, shipbuilding and overseas trade. For a long time there was no more trustworthy method of transport in the world than the Dutch canal barge. In times of need the Netherlander even enrolled the water as his ally. He barricaded himself behind the Hollandse Waterlinie, a wide stretch of flooded land, bordered with a series of fortifications. Water also had an important role in the protection of cities and fortresses.

The bond between the Netherlands and the water is eternal and indissoluble. The threat of flooding is less obvious than it used to be. Behind the proud Delta Works, designed to prevent catastrophes which statistically occur once in ten thousand years, a sense of safety reigns. And so the surprise was all the greater when, in 1995, the enemy attacked the Netherlands from behind and overflowing rivers prompted mass evacuations. In the Low Countries the message remains 'Watch out!', because despite his great knowledge of the water and his ability to control it, the Netherlander has never had, and never will have, webbed feet!

Above
In severe winters aquatic animals sometimes suffer from a lack of food, but not from the cold. An afternoon nap on the ice is just part of everyday life!

Below
The striking facades of the houses on the Zaanse Schans (North Holland) stare impassively out across the expanse of ice.

The church in Spijk, in the province of Groningen, seems to rise out of the water. Spijk is a splendid example of a terp village. 'Terp' means 'mound' and these structures were raised from 500 BC onwards by the Friesian population of the North Netherlands. These people had settled on small natural hillocks in the region where the land met the sea. As the sea level rose, the 'islands' had to be heightened from time to time. To some extent this occurred naturally through the accumulation of rubbish and manure, but there was plenty of clay about and it was also used for this purpose. Terps were sometimes as much as fifteen metres in height. Originally they would contain a single house, but gradually villages and even towns were built on them. Leeuwarden, the capital of Friesland, for example, was created from three terp villages.

In Friesland, Groningen and North Holland there were about a thousand of these 'refuges'. Many have been damaged or have disappeared – one reason being the excavation of the fertile soil. In Spijk the traditional structure of the terp village can still be clearly recognized. The houses and farms lie around the church, itself encircled by a canal, which stands on the terp's highest point.

17

Left
Typical Dutch winter scenes: having great fun on the ice in Woudsend in Friesland (above) **and the frozen harbour of the idyllic IJsselmeer village of Durgerdam, near Amsterdam** (below).

Right
Still water landscapes in Friesland: a windmill near Baburen (above) **and a watchful heron at Sint-Nicolaasga** (below).

Sailing vessels

In a land of wind and water sailing vessels like the lovely **Lemsteraak** (below right) **are a familiar sight. Among the most impressive are the four hundred or more ships of the 'Bruine Vloot' (Brown Fleet), which until the fifties were still employed in the fishing industry, the coastal trade and on inland waterways. The name refers to a traditional custom in inland navigation – tarring the sails, so they would last longer. When the fleet was modernized these sailing vessels – ranging from 'modest' tjalks to seagoing clippers and schooners – were pensioned off, but from the sixties onwards were restored to their former glory by private individuals. Now they are hired out to parties of passengers who want the experience of an 'old-fashioned' sail on the IJsselmeer, the Wadden Sea, the North Sea or the Friesian lakes. High points in the lives of the skippers are the annual sailing races, such as the Pieper race off Volendam** (middle). **The best known annual sailing event is the 'skûtsjesilen'** (far left, below), **a two-week regatta in Friesland for skûtsjes (tjalks) built in that province. The manifestation** SAIL **Amsterdam** (far left, middle), **organized every five years, attracts up to a thousand unique vessels, ranging from majestic windjammers to historic merchant vessels. The 'ijsschuit'** (far left, above) **is a typically Dutch invention, dating from the early 17th century. It was used to carry passengers and freight on frozen lakes and waterways and at that time was by far the fastest method of transport. The classic ijsschuit reached eighty kilometres per hour, modern versions as much as 140 kilometres per hour.**

Aquatic animals

Permanent inhabitants of the Dutch waters. From top left to bottom right: **mute swans, a green frog, seals, a grey heron, cormorants and a great crested grebe with chick. The seal is the least common of these creatures. About nine hundred of these endearing furry mammals live in the Wadden Sea, but you do not need to go to sea to see them. In the seal sanctuary in Pieterburen (Groningen) and the EcoMare Centre for the North Sea and Wadden Sea in De Koog (Texel), visitors can see how sick seals are cared for and, when they have recovered, how they are returned to the sea.**

The water as an ally. The fortress of Bourtange in the south-east of the province of Groningen, with its canals, ramparts, bastions and ravelins, is characteristically star-shaped. It was constructed during the 80-Years War (1568-1648), on the orders of the 'Father of Fatherlands' Prince William of Orange, on a sandy ridge ('tange') along which ran an important road to the city of Groningen, which at that time was occupied by Spanish troops. The 16th-century defensive work, originally occupied only by soldiers, attracted craftsman, farmers and traders and grew into a fortified town which reached its zenith half way through the 18th century. It fell into disrepair but in the second half of the 20th century it was beautifully restored to its 18th-century condition.

The struggle against the water

An eternal struggle against the water is the price the people of the Low Countries pay for their 'lowly' country. Nowhere is this better expressed than in the coat-of-arms of the province of Zeeland (above). 'I struggle and survive' is the province's motto. In order to keep his head above water the Netherlander was forced to become a specialist in hydraulic engineering. The terp (see pages 16-17) was the first milestone in this process; dike construction, after about 1000 AD, the second (below). The more modern works are examples of impressive engineering ingenuity. The Afsluitdijk (large photo), a thirty-kilometre-long link between the provinces of North Holland and Friesland, was completed in 1932. The Delta Works, a huge complex of dams and bridges protecting the delta region of the south-west, are world famous. The project was crowned in 1986 by the completion of the unique flood barrier in the Oosterschelde (second photo from top). The former artificial 'work' island Neeltje Jans is now a popular tourist attraction. The final piece of the Delta Works jigsaw is the flood barrier in the Nieuwe Waterweg, completed in 1997, and known as the 'eighth wonder of the world' (second photo from bottom). The two bow-shaped flood gates, which are closed in very bad weather, are the biggest moving mechanisms ever constructed. Including the hinge foundations, each of them is as long as the Eiffel Tower is high, and twice as heavy.

Above

New land. Large parts of the Netherlands have been re-claimed from the waters by impoldering. Originally, as in the case of the polders to the north of Amsterdam (right), this was done with the aid of wind-mills. In the 17th and 18th centuries the Netherlands was 'strewn' with windmills. The nineteen mills at Kinderdijk in the province of South Holland, in a typical polder landscape (middle), are a reminder of that time. These 18th-century windmills were used to pump water from the Alblasserwaard into the Lek. All except one are what are known as 'smock mills', mills with a rotating cap. Nowadays the windmill's work has been taken over by modern pumps. The Northeast Polder in the province of Flevoland (left) is one polder created with the aid of such pumps.

Below

'Boat farmers' at work in two characteristic 'water villages' in the province of Overijssel – transporting milk churns in Dwarsgracht (left and middle) and sheep in Giethoorn, the 'Venice of the North' (right). Both these places were originally settlements for peat cutters. This explains why the 'road network' consists of a series of canals – the dried peat was transported along them. The boat is still the prin-cipal form of transport; cars are striking by their absence.

Above
Dunes and beach at the popular seaside resort of Westkapelle in Zeeland.

Middle
The illuminated bridge over the Vecht, flanked by a Christmas tree, in rustic Vreeland in the province of Utrecht. Like many other places along the Vecht, in the 17th century this was a very popular country seat for wealthy Amsterdam merchants.

Below
The modern centre of Rotterdam. The Erasmus bridge spans the Nieuwe Maas. To the right is Noordereiland and the Willems bridge.

Above
Sailing ships of the Brown Fleet (see pages 20-21) **moored in the harbour of the old fishing village of Volendam (North Holland). This IJsselmeer town is very popular with tourists. In the Netherlands Volendam is famous as the source of very technically gifted footballers and as the cradle of several famous pop groups with their characteristic 'palingsound' – which literally translated means 'eel sound'.**

Middle
The Erasmus bridge in Rotterdam, also known as 'The Swan', a creation as elegant as it is daring. It fits perfectly into this bastion of modern and innovative architecture. Completed in 1996, the bridge is 808 metres long and its angled pylon pierces the sky to a height of 139 metres. It derives its name from the famous humanist Erasmus, who was born in Rotterdam in 1469. The city's university is also named after him.

Below
A characteristic view of Amsterdam, pre-eminently a 'city of water'. A series of concentric canals, which gives the town map the appearance of a spider's web, was gradually created around the dam on the river Amstel which gave the city its name. The centre dates from the Middle Ages and many of its canals – originally serving as defensive works, later as traffic routes – were filled in to suit the needs of modern forms of transport. In the photo are the Oude Schans and the Montelbaans tower, respectively part of the encircling canal system and city walls at the end of the 16th century.

Landscape

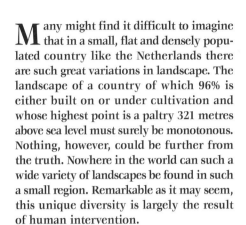

M any might find it difficult to imagine
that in a small, flat and densely populated country like the Netherlands there
are such great variations in landscape. The
landscape of a country of which 96% is
either built on or under cultivation and
whose highest point is a paltry 321 metres
above sea level must surely be monotonous.
Nothing, however, could be further from
the truth. Nowhere in the world can such a
wide variety of landscapes be found in such
a small region. Remarkable as it may seem,
this unique diversity is largely the result
of human intervention.

Unique versatility

The term 'Dutch landscape' immediately con-
jures up images of vast polders and grassy
meadows under high cloudy skies, as depicted
in the paintings of so many Dutch masters.
Perhaps we might also picture a landscape of
lakes dotted with white sails or one of the sand
dunes and broad beaches of the North Sea
coast. But we would certainly not imagine the
coniferous forests of the Veluwe, the heathlands of Drenthe or the hills and half-timbered
cottages of Limburg. Yet these landscapes are
just as 'Dutch' as the polders, the meadows,
the lakes and the sand dunes.
The most important characteristic of the Dutch
landscape is not the monotony people asso-

Page 32-33
Autumn in Het Gooi, a green, wooded region to the south-east of Amsterdam. Under the leafy roof of an avenue of beech trees, a cyclist wanders through the Spanderswoud, which lies between Hilversum, Bussum and 's-Graveland.
In the small photo are a pair of storks nesting in Groot-Ammers in South Holland. Over the years the number of storks had been dwindling and in 1969 a 'stork village' was successfully founded here in order to encourage their return.

Above and below
A relaxed barn owl (above) **and an industrious snail climbing against a background of poppies** (below).

ciate with a flat, green, watery land, but is actually its unusual variation. Given the small surface area of the country, this versatility is unique in the world. It is further enhanced by the changing of the seasons, which continually alters the aspect of the landscape. The enthusiast, then, will find much to enjoy in the Netherlands – considerably more than he might expect in a small, densely populated country. Nature itself has made its contribution, of course, but this unprecedented diversity is largely due to the work of the Netherlander who, over the centuries, has reshaped the contours of the land he lives in.

The influence of nature

In geologically terms the Dutch landscape is relatively young. It was largely created during the Ice Age and the Holocene period which followed it, and in which we still live. The simplest way to imagine the Netherlands is as a depression in the earth's crust which was gradually filled with sediment from the large rivers and the sea, debris transported by the land ice, and sand and loess carried by the wind.

All this resulted in a varied natural landscape. Besides extensive sandy regions in the east and south of the country, there are large areas of river and sea clays and peat and, in the far south-east, loess and chalky soils. Although in comparison with most other countries the Netherlands can quite rightly be called 'as flat as a pancake', there is a striking difference in height between the east ('high Netherlands') and the west ('low Netherlands'). The east is more than five metres above sea level, large areas of it even as much as twenty metres. There are also higher areas along the west coast - the sand dunes formed by the wind. These extend out across the seven Wadden islands to the north of the Dutch mainland. These islands, popular with beach enthusiasts, lovers of peace and quiet and those interested in plant and bird life, were once part of a long chain of dunes. The sea broke through and created the Wadden Sea which now separates the islands from the mainland.

Another characteristic feature of the landscape are the ridges, such as the Utrecht ridge and the Veluwe, which were forced up by the ice during the last ice age but one. The southern part of the province of Limburg, the far south-east of the country, is also hilly. This is a transitional region between the Belgian Ardennes and the Low Countries. Here, on the border with Belgium and Germany, lies the Vaalserberg, at a dizzying 321 metres the highest point of the Netherlands.

Cultivated landscape

But the influence of nature fades into insignificance when compared to the work of man, who shaped and recreated the natural landscape into one of order and cultivation. Originally the Netherlander adapted himself to the landscape, but as

the population grew and technological development progressed, he turned his attention to the 'wastelands'. He cut down the extensive forests of the sandy soils and drained the inaccessible marshes of the clay and peat regions. He dug out the peat, creating lakes, which were again partly drained. The result was a continually changing mosaic of man-made landscapes in which a rich variety of flora and fauna developed. Furthermore, man's intervention, both on land and sea, drastically changed the contours of the Netherlands; a comparison between old and modern maps makes this obvious at a glance.

In the past century this development has taken place at an increasing pace. An enormous growth in population – at the beginning of the century the Netherlands had about 5 million inhabitants, in 1997 some 15.5 million – went hand in hand with increasing prosperity and mobility, the scaling-up of agriculture, industrial expansion, a growing infrastructure and an increasing need for recreation, and resulted in a fundamental change in the use of space and the relationship between city and countryside. The Dutch landscape is a neatly ordered paradise, completely adapted to the needs of the people who live there. Just a few places, such as the unique nature reserve De Biesbosch, are reminiscent of the original natural state of the country.

The protected landscape

Over the course of time more and more Netherlanders became convinced that this far-reaching regulation of the landscape was taking place at the cost of the quality of life. It was not only the disappearance of 'free nature' that was regretted (at the most only four percent of the landscape can be so described), but there was also concern at the disappearance of characteristic landscape forms and species of plants and animals. In a country which has largely been created by human intervention such concern is perhaps a cause for wonder, but given the pace at which these changes have been completed it is very understandable. An additional factor is the toll taken by various forms of pollution.

This increasing concern is expressed in the growth of organizations for the protection of nature and the environment, which devote themselves to the conservation – and where possible the restoration – of nature and the landscape and to tackling the problem of pollution. Thanks partly to their efforts measures such as setting up nature reserves, protecting landscapes and planting forests have been taken. Species of animals – from certain breeds of cattle to beavers – which had disappeared from the Netherlands, have been reintroduced into their original habitats. Measures such as these are characteristic of the powerful 'we can make anything' mentality that marks out the Netherlander – if there is no 'free nature' left, then he will create it!

Left
An amorous tête-à-tête in a meadow in Almkerk in the province of North Brabant.

Above and below
Contrast in nature: the aggressive display of the pheasant (above) **and the phlegmatic attitude of the cow** (below).

Right
The Geuldal near Epen. The friendly, rolling landscape of South Limburg is literally a high point of the Low Countries. The hills form a transitional region between the Belgian Ardennes and the flat Netherlands. The half-timbered houses are also characteristic of this region.

Above and below
Well-known 'faces' of Dutch flora – the cultivated tulip and the wild poppy.

Conflicting interests

There is no doubt that the defenders of nature and landscape have achieved important successes, certainly in alerting the Netherlander to the unstable balance between quality of life and non-quality of life. It is partly due to them that in every respect the Netherlands is a country fit to live in, with a surprisingly large number of sparsely populated and beautiful spots where it is very pleasant to dwell.

Nonetheless 'quality of life' will always remain a matter of balancing interests – often conflicting ones. In such a densely populated country as the Netherlands, a land which also sets great store on prosperity and a high standard of living, tough choices are unavoidable. This dilemma is graphically illustrated by the furore over the plans for the construction of railway lines through the Betuwe and the so-called 'Green Heart' of the Randstad. This region, until now more or less untouched, lies literally at the heart of the great agglomeration which includes the large cities of Amsterdam, Rotterdam, The Hague and Utrecht. Yet another example is the debate concerning the rapid growth of Schiphol national airport, which can barely expand any further without creating unwarranted noise problems. Thoughts are therefore turning to the construction of a second airport, perhaps on an artificial island in the North Sea.

These examples clearly show that quality of life, almost by definition, is at odds with the desire or the necessity for economic growth. In a densely populated country like the Netherlands you simply cannot have your cake and eat it – even though you still have an unshakeable belief in your ability to create anything you want to create.

Above
**Summer in the Netherlands –
detail of a sunflower with wasp.**

Below
**Winter in the Netherlands –
vine leaves with hoarfrost.**

The Dutch landscape at its most recognizable – water, meadows, cows and a proud swan against a beautiful cloudy sky.

The four seasons

The wide variety of the Dutch landscape is enriched even more at the changing of the seasons. Each season stamps its mark on the landscape. Still snowscapes, like this one near Nigtevecht in the province of Utrecht (above left), are typical of winter. For most Netherlanders this is the season for skating and enjoying the cosiness of home, but many heave a sigh of relief – particularly after a long, hard winter – when the advent of spring colours the landscape; literally, in this field of rapeseed in Flevoland (below left). Summer reveals the Netherlands at its greenest. This is the season for those who enjoy typical scenes of green meadows and beautiful cloudscapes, as here in Brandeburen in Friesland (above right). Autumn, the season of falling leaves, has a charm all of its own. The woods in particular, with their wonderful colours and many species of fungi, have a fairy-tale feeling. The photo is of a coniferous forest in Ulvenhout in North Brabant (below right).

Flowers

The Netherlands is a land of flowers. People devote a great deal of attention to their gardens, where snowdrops appear before the end of winter (below right). Later in the year tulips, poppies and sunflowers form a familiar picture (left). At the beginning of May orchards in blossom in the fruit producing region of the Betuwe are a splendid sight. If the harvest is threatened by a late night frost, the growers spray the trees so that a protective layer of ice forms around the blossom (above right and right, middle). The bulb fields in flower are also worth seeing. These are the basis of a flourishing export trade, and also a popular tourist attraction. It is no wonder that throughout the world the Netherlands is associated with flowers – particularly with the tulip, a symbol for everything that is Dutch. In a certain sense, however, the Netherlands is displaying another man's finery – the tulip is not native to the country, but was imported from the Turkish Ottoman Empire in the 16th century. A wide variety of new species were cultivated in Western Europe from these imports. The Dutch word for tulip – 'tulp' – is itself imported, being derived from the Turkish word 'tulbend' (turban). At the end of April the Dutch bulb fields are reminiscent of a giant mosaic (middle). After they have flowered, the heads are cut off mechanically, a process that strengthens the bulbs and helps to ensure the Netherlands' blossoming reputation does not wither!

Sunrise in the Pettemer polder, North Holland.

Above left
Blooming heather on the Rechte Heide near Goirle in North Brabant. As in the province of Drenthe, extensive heathlands were created here in poor sandy soils as a consequence of the increase in the numbers of cattle, which were needed to provide fertilizer. The woodlands were a source of food for these and were gradually destroyed. They eventually made way for heathlands where large flocks of sheep were grazed. With the arrival of artificial fertilizer and cheap foreign wool both the heathlands and the sheep lost their function. In the 19th and 20th centuries the heathlands were largely converted to agricultural land and coniferous forests. Nowadays many of the remaining heathlands are protected.

Below left and above right
Autumn on the country estates of Jagtlust and Hilverbeek in 's-Graveland, North Holland. In the 17th century, rich Amsterdam merchants invested their profits in laying out country estates, where later they built beautiful country houses. The estates support an extremely varied plant and animal life and, together with the stately houses, farms, meadows and woods, they form a Mecca for lovers of nature and those who enjoy peace and quiet. A number of them are owned by the Natural Monuments Foundation, the Netherlands' largest organization for nature and landscape conservation, which has its headquarters in Schaep en Burgh, one of 's-Graveland's most prominent estates.

Below right
Fly agaric in a wood near Vught in North Brabant. This toadstool is extremely poisonous. Children claim that the pixies are immune to this poison, but the low number of sightings of this wood-dweller suggests otherwise!

Animals

A selection of typical country-side inhabitants proves that not only the landscape, but also animal life, has many facets. Some animals, moreover, have remarkable habits. In a lovely winter landscape near Boxtel in North Brabant, three sheep suspect there is something edible under the carpet of snow. Their thick fleece is useful in these conditions (above left). A misty meadow near Hilversum (North Holland) forms a lovely backcloth as two horses perform an unusual ballet (left, middle). In nearby Blaricum a herd of a rare breed of Dutch goat stare dreamily across the heathland (bottom left). This ancient Dutch species was almost extinct, but is once again making a contribution to the natural maintenance of the landscape. With this aim in mind still more animals are being released into their original habitat. Near the Zaanse Schans (North Holland) curious young belted cows – an indigenous species which, like the goat, was almost extinct – wonder what the photographer is up to (above right). In Andijk (North Holland) a goat has carefully selected a photogenic location (right, middle), while in a meadow in Meije (South Holland) a lamb gives an original interpretation to the concept of 'parental support' (bottom right).

Left
The romance of the woods: the Spanderswoud, which lies between Hilversum, Bussum and 's-Graveland. In prehistoric times there were extensive forests in the present provinces of North and South Holland, in fact there were throughout the Netherlands. The name 'Holland' was probably derived from this 'holt land' (woodland). In the 17th century the province of Holland (at that time it still had not been divided into North and South Holland) played a dominant role in the then Republic of the Seven United Provinces. This is the reason why nowadays the Netherlands is still frequently referred to as 'Holland'. Over the course of time these extensive forests made way for agricultural land and heathlands. For a long time the Netherlands even had fewer woodlands than almost any other country in Europe. But thanks to nature conservation and replanting the situation has now greatly improved.

Above right
Willows along a country road at Oosthuizen in North Holland.

Right, middle
Sunrise; a meadow in Blauwhuis in Friesland.

Below right
A man exercises his dog on the mud flats near the island of Ameland. At low water large parts of the Wadden Sea – the inland sea between the Wadden islands and the mainland – are dry. When the weather is good it is even possible to cross the Wadden Sea on foot – accompanied by a guide, of course.

The structures

Dutch towns and villages are just as efficiently arranged as the surrounding countryside, but what is particularly striking is the lack of any large metropolis. In the eyes of most foreigners even the big cities are no more than provincial towns, though they do have a strong cosmopolitan and historic character. Many people think it is the authentic combination of 'smallness' and character that gives the Netherlands its charm. Nevertheless, modern Dutch architecture is attracting increasing international attention, too.

A miniature country

Many foreigners are of the opinion that everything in the Netherlands is on a small scale, beginning with the country itself. According to international criteria even the cities are tiny – the biggest city in the Netherlands, Amsterdam, has only 715,000 inhabitants. Dutch buildings are also relatively small, in any event, low. Tall buildings are comparatively scarce – there are practically no skyscrapers whatsoever. Finally, many think Dutch houses and gardens are extremely cramped. But it is all a matter of what you are used to. The Dutch

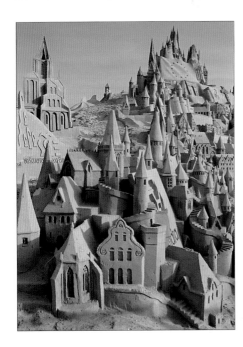

Page 52-53
The Brouwersgracht in Amsterdam, one of the many canals that are the trademark of the city. The canal dates from the 'golden' 17th century, when Amsterdam was the trading centre of the world. The original city dates from the Middle Ages, but at the beginning of the 17th century, due to an enormous growth in the population, it was forced to expand. Three parallel main canals were planned outside the walls and powerful merchants built their houses there. The warehouses were built on subsidiary side canals, one of which was Brouwersgracht. This ring of canals has maintained much of its ambiance and attracts visitors from all over the world. Seven thousand listed monuments lie within the ring, including a large number of canal houses. They reflect the status of the merchants, but also demonstrate their relatively sober lifestyle. There is little gaudy facade decoration, although the houses do have characteristic gables. Many of the buildings on Brouwersgracht have what are known as stepped gables, typical of the oldest type of canal house.
Small photo: **On the beach at Scheveningen (South Holland) today's master builders can indulge themselves during the annual International Sand Castle Festival.**

themselves, even though they are among the tallest people in the world, think they are fine! They are only surprised by the small scale of their country when they visit Madurodam, a miniature model 'city' in which most of the buildings are no more than knee-high.

The oldest structures

The oldest structures in the Netherlands are in the thinly-populated province of Drenthe. They are 53 communal megalithic tombs, called 'hunebedden', and they were erected from 3,000 BC onwards by the farming community. They consist of enormous granite boulders and vary in length from seven to about twenty -five metres. The largest is near the hamlet of Borger.

Later inhabitants left less impressive traces, but they were responsible for founding the first towns and villages. At the beginning of the Christian era the Romans established settlements in dozens of places along the Rhine and the Maas. They called the crossing places in these rivers 'traiectum', and it was from this word that names of cities such as Utrecht and Maastricht were derived.

Historic cities

Utrecht and Maastricht are among the many Dutch cities which are small according to international standards, but nonetheless extremely charming and historically interesting. Historic towns and cities which are well worth seeing include Amsterdam, Utrecht, The Hague, Maastricht, Groningen, Leiden, Delft, Gouda, Haarlem, Deventer, Zutphen, Zwolle, Kampen, Gouda, Hoorn, Enkhuizen, Naarden, Buren and Middelburg. Not only the towns themselves, but also their museums – the Netherlands has the highest 'density' of museums in the world – offer the visitor a detailed picture of the past.

The development of several cities, including Amsterdam, can still be traced. A canal would be dug around the historic heart, building would take place outside it and this extension to the city would again be encircled by a canal. Some towns were also enclosed by ramparts, walls and bastions for defence. A limited number of bridges and gates gave access to these places, which sometimes took the form of a real fortress, characteristically in the form of a star. The most splendid example is the town of Bourtange. Over the centuries, and particularly since the emergence of motorized traffic, characteristic historical elements have disappeared from many townscapes. In Utrecht – in the Middle Ages for a long time the largest city in the Netherlands – many of the canals were filled in to facilitate the construction of roads and shopping centres. It has now been decided to restore these canals to their former glory. The current trend is to banish cars from the inner cities.

Modern cities

Rotterdam – the world's largest seaport – is a surprising omission from the list of historic cities. At the beginning of the Second World War it was largely destroyed by German air raids and today it is a classic example of a 'modern' city. It is no coincidence that the Netherlands Architectural Institute is established here – in a quite remarkable building in which exhibitions dedicated to modern architecture are held. Spectacular modern buildings can be found on the Kop van Zuid, the Weena, along the Maasboulevard, and in many other places in the city.

Those who enjoy rather older architecture can still find a few interesting buildings which survived the bombardment. Hotel New York, as splendid as it is popular, and situated in the former head office of the illustrious Holland-America Line, is a famous example. The Van Nelle factory, a wonderful example of the architectural style known as 'Het Nieuw Bouwen' (New Building) is another.

The new towns built on reclaimed land in the polders are also world renowned. The best examples are Almere and Lelystad, dating from the sixties and planned down to the last paving stone. Experimental ideas in building and living were given free rein here and Almere, in particular, has much to offer in the field of modern architecture. The central role given to public transport in the infrastructure of both these towns is another striking feature.

Other modern architecture

The Netherlands has much splendid 20th-century architecture. Housing and office developments, bridges, stadiums and other constructions have attracted international admiration. Dutch Railways, which has produced dozens of much talked-about designs for railway stations, must also be mentioned in this context. In addition, there is a large number of striking buildings in styles which are never, or only rarely, seen outside the Netherlands. In particular, there is increasing appreciation for buildings from the 1910-1930 period, designed by Berlage and representatives of two prominent movements, the Amsterdam School and 'De Stijl' (The Style).

Berlage, one of the Netherlands' most famous architects, achieved international recognition and was the inspiration and pioneer of modern Dutch architecture. His buildings are simple and functional and built in brick. Among his best-known designs are the Commodity Exchange on the Damrak in Amsterdam (1903), the Sint Hubertus hunting lodge in the Hoge Veluwe (1920) and the Gemeentemuseum (Municipal Museum) in The Hague (1935).

Architects of the Amsterdam School were also fond of using brick. In contrast to the simplicity of Berlage's work, this movement is noted for its highly imaginative designs. Brick was often only used in the towers, decorative doorways and fanciful curved features in the facade, behind which was a rigid design in concrete. Spectacular buildings of the Amsterdam School can still be admired in many places and are increasingly being designated as listed monuments. Examples are Van der Mey's Scheepvaarthuis (Shipping House) in Amsterdam (1916), De Klerk's

Left
The commodore's houses in Nes in Ameland (above) are reminders of the island's fishing and seagoing history. Whalers, under the command of a commodore, sailed from here in the 17th and 18th centuries. The typical green houses of Marken, a former fishing village on the IJsselmeer and a popular destination for tourists (below).

Middle
A 'hunebed' (megalithic tomb) in Havelte in Drenthe (above). The 'hunebedden' are the oldest monuments in the Netherlands. The graves, built of 'erratic blocks' (boulders transported from what is now Scandinavia during the second last Ice Age), were originally covered with earth.
A street scene in Nes, the main village on the Wadden island of Ameland (middle).
The lovely centre of Middelburg, encircled by a canal and bastions (below). For centuries, the provincial capital of Zeeland was an important trading centre and was the home of branches of the Dutch East Indies Company and the West Indies Company (see also page 67).

Above and below
The 'Vredespaleis' (Peace Palace) in The Hague, completed in 1913, which houses the International Court of Justice (above). The skyline of the Zeeland resort of Westkapelle (below).

Right
See the Netherlands in a couple of hours? This is possible in the miniature city of Madurodam in The Hague. On a scale of 1:25, Madurodam gives a fascinating image of 'the structured Netherlands'. Dozens of imposing buildings and city quarters, ranging from windmills to examples of modern architecture, have been carefully 'rebuilt'. Madurodam was founded in 1952 with money donated by the parents of the Dutch-Antillian George Maduro, who died in a German concentration camp in 1945.

Above
A farm in the polder landscape in the province of Flevoland.

Below
The harbour of Hoorn in North Holland with its 16th century Hoofdtoren (see also page 59). **From the 14th to the 18th century Hoorn was a prosperous trading and fishing port. The Dutch East India Company, the West India Company and the Northern Company all established branches here. Wandering through the lovely old harbour, you can almost imagine yourself being carried back to the days when Hoorn was a rich and important trading centre.**

public housing in Amsterdam's Spaarndammer-buurt (1918) and Kramer's Bijenkorf department store in The Hague (1926), as well as many bridges, country houses and villas in Bergen and Het Gooi, among other places.

A completely different perspective was held by a group of artists known as 'De Stijl', who propagated abstract design, based on straight lines and the use of only a few colours. The group included the painter Mondriaan, the painter-architect Van Doesburg, and architects such as J.J.P. Oud, Rietveld, Van 't Hoff and Wils. Their most famous buildings include the Rietveld-Schröder house in Utrecht (1924) and Oud's De Unie café in Rotterdam (1925).

The countryside

There is also much to enjoy architecturally in the Dutch countryside. There are more than 3,000 villages in the Netherlands and a remarkable variety of village types – a phenomenon linked to the great variation in landscape forms. For example, there are coastal villages, terp villages built on mounds, villages built round central squares and ribbon villages. Despite modernization, in many places the original link between village and landscape can still be clearly seen. This also applies to local architectural differences. In scores of villages fixed colour combinations and particular materials were used. Examples of these can be found along the IJsselmeer and in the Zaanstreek, among other places.

Farms and windmills, very 'Dutch' constructions which are found particularly in the countryside, come in all shapes and sizes. The most important types can be seen in the Open Air Museum in Arnhem, which gives an imposing picture of life in the countryside. This museum is a true paradise for visitors who want to taste the authentic charm and 'smallness' of the Netherlands.

Above

With its neat gardens and fairy-tale towers the castle of De Haar in Haarzuilens (Utrecht) looks rather like a scale model. This castle, dating from the 14th and 15th centuries, went up in flames in the 17th century but was rebuilt in 1892. During this work the village which in the meantime had grown up around the ruins was demolished and rebuilt further away.

Middle

The village of Zuiderwoude to the north of Amsterdam, lying in polderland with the appropriate name 'Waterland', is situated on a terp, now surrounded by trees.

Below

Veere, in Zeeland, is a small town with a great history. The 13th-century fishing village quickly grew into an important port and trading centre, particularly after it became a depot for Scottish wool in the 16th century. There is much to remind us of this period in the inner city, including the Town Hall with its imposing tower and the robust Great Church, both clearly recognizable in the photo. Around 1800 trading came to an end and Veere again became a fishing port. The construction of the Delta works dealt a death blow to fishing and nowadays the harbour is the domain of watersports enthusiasts, enjoying themselves on the Veerse Meer.

Above

Sturdy yet elegant, Nijenrode castle resists Jack Frost. This 13th-century former knight's manor house near Breukelen in Utrecht has had its share of warmer times – it was a football in the struggle between the Bishops of Utrecht and the Counts of Holland, and destroyed by the French. In 1946 it was handed over to students (among them this photographer) and became a training institute. It is now a university. Nevertheless, Nijenrode is one of the loveliest castles in the country.

Middle

A winter idyll in Friesland: Sloten – or Sleat as it is known in Friesian (parts of the Netherlands are bilingual) – is one of those places that can truly be called 'picturesque'. Though small (650 inhabitants) Sloten was an important defensive town in the 16th century. Remains of the defensive works can still be seen. Some of the houses along the village canal date from the 17th and 18th centuries.

Below

The harbour of Hoorn (North Holland) and the Hoofdtoren, which was part of the 16th-century defensive works encircling the city, and later housed the Northern Company, a whaling concern. For a long time this former Zuider Zee port was a formidable competitor to Amsterdam as a trading centre. In around 1725 one in three of the male inhabitants was a seaman and the same number worked in businesses linked to trading. The warehouses and offices also offered work to many. The Dutch East India Company was the biggest employer at that time.

The atmospheric Voldersgracht in Delft in the province of South Holland. It is believed that the famous artist Johannes Vermeer was born here in 1632. Whether this is true or not, the fame of Delft – which in any event was a great source of inspiration for the painter who was far from famous when he was alive – is none the less for it. A more doubtful milestone in the history of Delft was the murder of William of Orange, the leader in the struggle for an independent Netherlands, in 1584. The 'Father of the Fatherland' is buried in the Nieuwe Kerk (New Church). Nearby, in the Oude Kerk (Old Church), lie other prominent victims of these stirring times, the naval heroes Piet Hein and Maarten Tromp. Hein was born in Delfshaven, Delft's seaport, later swallowed by Rotterdam, and worked for the West India Company which, like the Dutch East India Company, had offices in the city. Overseas trade was indirectly responsible for the city's fame. Chinese porcelain imported from East Asia was the source of inspiration for the china industry which went on to provide the whole of Europe with 'Delft Blue'. This china is still the Delft's trademark, although the original Asian motifs have long been replaced by the characteristic cityscapes which make Delft one of the most beautiful historical cities in the Netherlands.

The Big Four

There are four 'big' cities in the Netherlands – Amsterdam (715,000 inhabitants), Rotterdam (600,000), The Hague (445,000) and Utrecht (235,000). All four are part of what is known as the 'Randstad', a huge agglomeration in the West of the country, where the largest part of the population lives. Although they are not very far apart, each of these cities has its own distinctive character.

Utrecht is the least known of the four. It was originally a Roman town. In the Middle Ages it was the seat of a powerful bishopric and a prosperous trading centre, and for long afterwards an important fortified town. The atmospheric canals and ramparts in the centre date from this period. Oudegracht (large photo) is in the heart of the city and its banks were lined by buildings as early as 1200. Between 1300 and 1500 the wharves, characteristic of the Utrecht canals, were built. These were linked to the canal houses by deep cellars. These restored wharves and cellars, with their restaurants, bars and pavement cafés, play an important role in the leisure life of the city. Utrecht's most eye-catching feature is the 14th-century, 112 metre tall, Domtoren, the tallest church tower in the country.

Rotterdam, as befits a seaport, is known as a city of hard workers whose motto is 'not words, but deeds'. Rotterdam is also the most modern city in the Netherlands, a focus of modern architecture which is not afraid to experiment (see pages 74-75). Since the dramatic German bombardment of May 1940, which destroyed the entire centre of the city, Rotterdam appears to have been in the grip of a 'new building virus'. But the ambiance of old Rotterdam – for example, the Veerhaven (above) – can still be found here and there, nestling between modern constructions like the Erasmus bridge (small photo left).

The Hague, the 'lovely city behind the sand dunes', is the seat of government and the most stately city in the country. The beautiful palaces and houses and great squares have an unmistakable air of distinction. Although impressive new building projects are taking up increasing space, the centre still has the ambiance of the days when the Counts of Holland established their courts there. The photo (middle) shows the 17th-century Mauritshuis (left), now a world-famous museum housing a unique collection of paintings, and part of the Binnenhof (right), the seat of government and parliament. The little tower in the centre houses the Prime Minister's office.

The capital city, Amsterdam, with its relatively old centre, is a historical open air museum, with monumental canal houses and about a thousand bridges – probably more than any other city in the world. The 17th-century Magere Brug – 'Skinny bridge' – (below), spanning the Amstel, is the most famous. The ambiance in the city is free and democratic. The typical Amsterdammer is open, humorous and self-confident; 'arrogant', they say in arch-rival Rotterdam.

Above
Living in the countryside: Kortenhoef in the province of North Holland.

Middle
The Kurhaus in the seaside resort of Scheveningen (South Holland) is a fashionable hotel dating from 1885. Six months after it was opened it went up in flames, but the damage was repaired in record time. It was fundamentally renovated in the seventies.

Below
The 14th-century Zuidhaven- poort (left) and the 15th-cen- tury Noordhavenpoort (right) in Zierikzee, two of the three gates of this Zeeland town which have stood the test of time. The cupola on the roof of the Zuidhavenpoort houses the oldest working carillon in the country. Zierikzee was an important trading centre and seaport as early as the 13th century and it remained so until the 18th. Time then stood still until the first tourists knocked on the city gates in the 1970's. The part of the city inside the canals, dating from the Middle Ages, has remained largely unchanged.

Above
The Netherlands is rich in water, but not many Netherlanders can afford a house by the water and a boat outside the front door.

Middle
The country estate of Trompenburgh in 's-Graveland, North Holland. The house dates from 1680 and was the property of Admiral Cornelis Tromp, who even in the middle of the Gooise greenery wanted to see the water from his living room. The house was built in the form of a ship and crowned with a model of Tromp's ship De Witte Olifant (The White Elephant). The statues in the niches above the waterline mostly represent Roman gods. Trompenburgh is the loveliest of the many country houses built in 's-Graveland in the 17th century. The builders were rich Amsterdam merchants who saw the laying out of country estates as a profit-making enterprise. Originally they only visited their estates to show their faces or to collect the rents from their farms. But country life beguiled them and they decided to build country houses, far from the stresses of the city jungle. They surrounded their houses, naturally, by parkland and provided them with stables, a coach house, a teahouse and all the other things so desperately needed in the countryside. One even had a zoo containing four hundred exotic animals. Opposite them the ribbon village of 's-Graveland was created. In the first instance this consisted of a long row of buildings housing service industries, including a remarkable number of laundries; after all, it was easy to get splattered in mud while riding around your country estate!

Below
The famous Amsterdam canal houses seem to rise from the water like islands.

Facade decoration

The striking gable forms (above) are a charming feature of canal houses in Amsterdam – and in other places, too. The earliest type is what is known as the 'stepped gable' (the house far left in the photo). Later they acquired the form of a 'neck' (far right) and, as a playful variation, a 'bell' (second right). The 18th century brought greater unity; a row of gables was now uniform. Many 17th-century gables were also adapted and therefore a relatively modern gable might conceal a much older house. Warehouses usually have a simple triangular gable, the so-called 'cornet gable', and can also be recognized by their wooden shutters.

A second striking element of the facades are the stone tablets which made a general appearance in the 17th century. However beautiful or original, these tablets were not only intended as decoration – there were no street signs and house numbers and they functioned as name boards and addresses, picturing the name or profession of the person living in the house, or the name of the house. One beautiful example is the stone with a depiction of a 'bonte koe' (mottled cow) in Hoorn (below) which decorates the house in which Willem IJsbrantsz. Bontekoe was born. Bontekoe was a privateer sailing the seas in his ship De Bontekoe. He later entered the service of the Dutch East India Company. He wrote a book about these experiences which became a best-seller. As a Hoorn maritime hero, his only competitors are Jan Pietersz. Coen (governor of the Dutch East India Company) and Pieter Cornelisz. Schouten, the man who named the most southerly tip of America – Cape Horn – after his home town.

Above left
The stately, richly-ornamented Town Hall of Middelburg (Zeeland), designed by two Belgian architects in 1452 and inspired by the City Hall of Brussels, which had just been completed. The niches between the windows on the first floor contain statues of the Counts and Countesses of Zeeland. Like the rest of the historic centre of Middelburg, this building was destroyed by German bombs in May 1940. It was rebuilt in its original form – a quite remarkable feat.

Above right
The 14th-century spire of the former Town Hall of Zierikzee in the province of Zeeland. The wooden crown and the figure of Neptune date from the early 16th century.

Below left
A winter view of the Muiderslot in North Holland. This sturdy 13th-century stronghold is particularly well-known for its most famous inhabitant – the poet, writer and historian P.C. Hooft. In the first half of the 17th century, Hooft surrounded himself with men of letters, historians and artists – the Muiderkring (Muider circle). The Muiderslot is now a museum.

Below right
Sailing ships, moored in front of elegant canal houses in Amsterdam.

Architecture 1915-1940

The main post office in Utrecht is an imposing building which, had it had been situated elsewhere, might well be world famous. It was built in 1917-1924 to the design of J. Crouwel jr., in the tradition of the Amsterdam School.

Page 70
The Museum Boymans Van Beuningen in Rotterdam (above left) was built in 1928-1935 to the design by A. van der Steur. The Town Hall of Hilversum in North Holland (above right), completed in 1931, is W.M. Dudok's best-known work and shows the influence of two important architectural movements, the Amsterdam School and 'Het Nieuwe Bouwen' (The New Building). The St. Hubertus hunting lodge in the Hoge Veluwe national park in the province of Gelderland (below left) was designed by the famous architect H.P. Berlage and was completed in 1920. The design was inspired by the legend of St. Hubertus and his meeting with a deer which had an illuminated cross in its antlers. The ground plan is in the form of antlers. It was commissioned by the Kröller-Müllers, whose land and art collection formed the basis for the national park and the Rijksmuseum Kröller-Müller which lies within it. The world-famous Rietveld-Schröder house in Utrecht (below right), completed in 1924, is to the radical design by G. Rietveld. It is a classic example of the architecture of De Stijl.

Page 71
Ventilation building for the Maas tunnel in Rotterdam, designed by A. van der Steur and completed in 1942 (above). Round 1915-1920 a number of interesting houses in the style of the Amsterdam School were erected in the Spaarndammerbuurt in Amsterdam (below).

Modern architecture

The Amsterdam ArenA (above), designed by S. Soeters and R. Schuurman, and the home of Ajax football club. The entrance to the miniature city of Madurodam in The Hague, the work of A. Bhalotra (middle). Light art by P. Struycken in the arcade under the Netherlands Architectural Institute in Rotterdam (below). Detail of the Groninger Museum, the product of a group of architects led by A. Mendini (small photo).

Page 73
Modern high-rise buildings, as seen from the Maritiem Buitenmuseum (Open Air Maritime Museum) in Rotterdam (large photo). The Gas Union's office in Groningen, designed by Alberts and Van Huut (above). Detail of the 'Haagse Arc' in The Hague, designed by F. Temme and housing PTT Telecom (middle). Holland Casino Scheveningen, designed by P. de Bruijn (below).

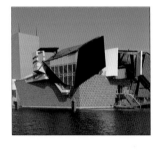

Page 74-75
Almost by definition, Rotterdam is a city of builders. Since the city centre was destroyed by German bombs in May 1940 – an event symbolised by the 1953 statue 'The Destroyed City' by Ossip Zadkine, which depicts a despairing man whose heart has been torn out (above) – the city has been feverishly building towards its future. The large photo shows office buildings and flats and, to the right, the 17th-century Schielandshuis which houses the Historical Museum.
An office building in the city centre (below) and the famous cubic apartments on the Blaak, designed by P. Blom (middle).

The people

'**T**ypically Dutch!' we foreigners exclaim in exasperation. 'Typically Dutch!' say the Dutch with pride. There are 15.5 million Netherlanders and almost as many stereotypes. Although there is undoubtedly an element of truth in each, put together they give only a vague impression of the real Netherlander. In fact, the 'typical Dutchman' probably does not exist, though we can point to a number of qualities which are characteristic of 'Homo Neerlandicus'.

A well-ordered paradise

A foreigner arriving in the Netherlands by plane learns one fundamental characteristic of the Netherlander before he even lands. Below him a model of order and regularity unfurls; a patchwork quilt of fields and meadows, divided by waterways, straight as arrows, and villages and housing estates laid out with geometric precision. It is immediately obvious that in designing his country the Netherlander has left nothing to chance. With a passion for organization he has created a neat, well-ordered paradise.

In an overcrowded country – the Netherlands is one of the most densely populated in the world – a talent for organization is an absolute necessity. And for centuries the country's geographical location made great demands on these powers of organization. This land, at the mercy of the whims of the sea, was like a house declared unfit to live in. Restoring and maintaining it demanded co-operation and consultation and stimulated the Netherlander to carry out his dealings in an orderly and precise manner. There is no doubt that the character of the Netherlander was largely determined by his country's extraordinary geographical circumstances.

Page 76-77
A mime artist entertains passers-by on the Dam in the centre of Amsterdam. Small photo: **detail of a street organ.**

Above
Clogs, traditional costume and a bicycle – the stereotype Netherlander to life! A musician in the show band Crescendo.

Page 79
Self portrait, painted in 1887, of Vincent van Gogh (1853-1890), perhaps the most famous Netherlander of all. His very personal and powerful work appeals to everybody's imagination. And, of course, the story of his life reads like a grand drama. The suicide of this unhappy, emotional man undoubtedly contributed to his fame, but more important is the undisputed quality of his extensive oeuvre, which was created in only ten years. In Arles (France) during the last two years of his life alone he made more than four hundred paintings. The brilliant use of colour in these later works forms a sharp contrast with his somewhat sober early work. Van Gogh often asked himself what the point of his work was. The answer to that question is now very obvious – Van Gogh was one of the most important founders of modern art. The collections in the Van Gogh Museum in Amsterdam and the Kröller-Müller Museum in Otterlo in the province of Gelderland give a good overall view of his work.

The world his back garden

The Netherlander owes his spirit of enterprise and his international orientation to these same circumstances. He quickly learned to regard the sea not only as an enemy, but also as a source of income and as a means of communication. The Netherlander was a fisherman but, in particular, he was a trader. The geographical position of the Netherlands by the North Sea and at the deltas of three large rivers marked him out for commerce and he entered his vocation with conviction. The world was his back garden and during the 17th century the tiny Netherlands dominated global trade.

The modern-day Netherlander has much in common with the successful 17th-century merchant. He is enterprising and very internationally oriented; he is punctual, fair, practical, sober, hospitable and trustworthy, qualities which are of the utmost importance in the business world. He also communicates easily, he is informal and just as accessible as his own flat country, and because of his great talent for languages he is also – quite literally – easy to approach. These qualities make the Netherlander a much-desired partner internationally. They also explain why such a tiny country as the Netherlands is so strongly represented on the international stage in economics, politics and culture, as well as sport.

A builder of bridges

His inbred tolerance is another essential quality that the Netherlander finds useful internationally. He is accustomed to respecting other people's individuality and to seeking compromise when interests clash, rather than insisting on having his own way, cost what it may. The Netherlander is a bridge builder, not only literally but also metaphorically, and he sees it as self-evident that this attitude demands a certain flexibility.

In the overcrowded Netherlands an ability to adapt and tolerance are vital, but these qualities, too, are deeply rooted in the common struggle against the sea and in the commercial past. The water's threat taught the Netherlander to subordinate himself to the common interest; those who did not temper their pigheadedness were guaranteed, sooner or later, to get their feet wet – or worse! And pragmatic as they were, the 17th-century merchants quickly saw the value of tolerance. After all, trade only thrives in a climate of freedom and mutual respect, and for the merchant a customer is a customer, irrespective of the colour of his skin or his beliefs.

A tolerant nation

The attitude of 'live and let live' is deeply embedded in the Dutch psyche; so much so that in the first half of the 20th century Dutch society 'split', as it were, into four segments, or socio-political groupings – Catholic, Reformed, socialist and neutral – each with its own ideological character. These groups had their own political parties, trade unions, schools, broadcasting organizations, societies, hospitals and newspapers and for many Netherlanders the world they lived in was largely limited to their own group. This unique phenomenon became much less important after 1950 under the influence of increasing secularization, emancipation and prosperity.

A second far-reaching consequence of Dutch tolerance was that throughout the centuries countless immigrants found their way to the Netherlands. At the end of the 16th century almost half the population of Amsterdam consisted of foreigners. A large part of today's Dutch population is descended from immigrants. The many 'foreign' names in the phone book – Hirsch Ballin, d'Ancona, Ritzen, Dreesmann, Lopes Dias, Collet, Blangé, Cohen – bear witness to this. The flames under the great melting pot of Dutch society have been rekindled in recent decades by the arrival of a large number of immigrants from former colonies and Mediterranean countries.

The Netherlands is still internationally recognized as a liberal and tolerant nation. Many are even of the opinion that the Netherlands is a country where anything goes. They refer to the famous Dutch 'tradition of tolerance', which is being increasingly copied internationally, and in particular they cite the great number of coffee shops, where not much coffee is drunk but where there is a flourishing trade in other mind-expanding products. Although this view is greatly exaggerated, it is certainly true that to a large extent people can do as they want to in the Netherlands.

Good company

How ever exceptional they might have been, the Netherlander is unassuming about his achievements. Ostentation is strange to him. He is sober, calm and thorough and prefers moderation and simplicity to pomp and circumstance. "Just be ordinary, that's mad enough", is an old Dutch saying. Those who do not conform to this are soon regarded as being 'over the top'!

Even the Dutch Royal Family is ordinary. There is not much distance between Queen Beatrix ('Bea', as the people call her) and her subjects. In other kingdoms Bea's modest palace would probably be used to house the royal ceremonial coaches. Crown Prince Willem-Alexander ('Alex') also does his best to be ordinary. If the monarch-in-waiting sprints jubilantly across a sports field the man in the street grumbles that he is just a bit too ordinary and that, too, is 'over the top'.

The ordinary Netherlander is not renowned for being a born reveller. Sometimes he is even imputed to be rather surly and lacking in spontaneity. He is called a stay-at-home and – with reference to the Dutch climate – a cold fish.

The tourist who – this description in mind – arrives in the Netherlands on the Queen's Birthday or when an important sporting event is taking place, will wonder whether he has not got on the wrong plane. The exuberance generated on such occasions by a merrymaking multitude of stay-at-homes and cold

Right and below
All blessings come from on high, grumbles the Nether-lander, as yet again the rain pours down profusely on his head. Seldom has this lamen-tation been more true than during the 'Grote Ommegang' (Great Procession) in Maastricht. This procession marks the end of the 'Heiligdomsvaart', a ten-day-long Catholic celebration which is held once every seven years. Holy relics, including those of the patron saint of the city, Saint Servaas, are carried in the procession.

Above
Relaxing in the big city; tai-chi in the Vondel park in Amsterdam.

fish is strongly reminiscent of a Brazilian carnival. It is true that the Netherlander spends a lot of time indoors, but that is mainly forced upon him – he who does not take account of the weather is asking for trouble. But social life is no less intense because of it. There is a huge number of clubs and associations, and the many places of entertainment are generally well-filled. Moreover, Netherlanders frequently visit each other. Usually by appointment, true, but that is largely out of respect for each other's privacy. When the weather allows life moves outside. In the summer months the pavement cafés are packed until late in the evening.

Just how companionable the Netherlander is can be seen from the attention he pays to his house and garden. There, with great care and devotion, he creates his very own, well-ordered paradise.

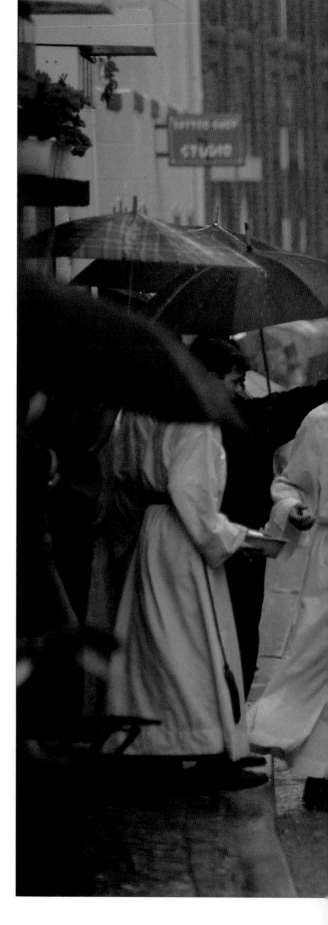

Above left
A girl from Marken in North Holland in local costume. The Netherlands has a rich costume tradition. Particular attention was paid to women's lace caps and cap brooches. In the 20th century the wearing of local and district costume fell out of use. In only a few places, particularly Marken and Staphorst, and to a lesser degree Urk, Spakenburg, Bunschoten, Volendam, Scheveningen (above right) and a few places in Zeeland, is the tradition still honoured. Elsewhere traditional costume has now become part of the local folklore.

Above right
Head back, this Scheveningen woman demonstrates how herring should be eaten. Most foreigners shudder at the thought that many Netherlanders regard raw herring as a delicacy. For preference the fish should be lightly salted and eaten with chopped onion.

Below left
Dressed to kill at the cheese market in Edam, North Holland.

Below right
A captivating Antillian girl in Amsterdam, all dressed up for the party. In recent decades the majority of inhabitants of foreign extraction have come to the Netherlands from the former colonies (the Dutch East Indies, Surinam and the Dutch Antilles) or as guest workers from Mediterranean countries (particularly Morocco and Turkey). Together with their families, they form about six percent of the population, but there is a much higher percentage in cities such as Amsterdam, Rotterdam and The Hague.

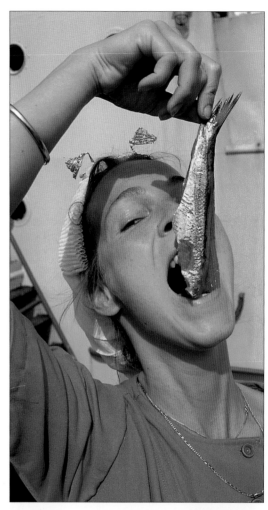

Contemplative glances: a cheese porter at the cheese market in Edam (above left); a reed cutter near Ossenzijl in Overijssel (above right); a miller at Zaanse Schans in North Holland (below left) and a cheese maker near Edam in North Holland (below right).

Unusual professions

The street organ, a musical instrument which is as much a part of Amsterdam as the canals (right). The popularity of tunes such as 'Tulips from Amsterdam' and 'On the Amsterdam canals' is largely due to the organ grinders, who accompany the strident music with the rattle of a 'centenbak' in which passers-by deposit coins. The barrel organ was originally an instrument for the aristocracy and later for the wealthy citizen. It appeared in cafés and on the streets in the 19th century. Outside the Netherlands it has almost disappeared. The street organ in the photo is one of the oldest in Amsterdam and the grinder himself is conducting the music.
Other familiar sights in the centre of Amsterdam are patrolling policemen on skeelers – the Amsterdam police keep

up with the times! – (small photo) and intellectuals beavering away on houseboats (page 85, right). According to recent figures there are approximately 2500 houseboats on the canals of Amsterdam – though not all of them are inhabited by intellectuals!

Unusual activities in the countryside. Reed cutters at work in the De Weerribben national park in the province of Overijssel, an extensive region of meadows, marshlands and reed-lands, created by the cutting of peat (above). In the winter months some twenty professional growers cut 'the best roofing thatch in Europe'. The profession is traditionally passed down from father to son and is generally combined with another occupation – cattle farming, for example.
A shepherd on the Drenthe heathlands near Exloo (middle). The sandy soils of Drenthe were once thickly wooded. The soil became poor due to intensive deforestation and over-grazing by cattle, which led to the creation of extensive heathlands on which huge herds of sheep were kept, providing fertilizer for the fields. The invention of artificial fertilizer and the import of cheap wool reversed the situation; heathlands were reclaimed as agricultural land or for tree planting and many herds of sheep disappeared from the

landscape. Today, some of the heathlands which exist are protected. Sheep are still widely farmed in the neighbourhood of Exloo, however, and this village has its own 'communal' herd.
The photographer of this book, here in conversation with a calf, is the odd one out in the countryside (below).

Cycling

Almost by definition the Netherlands is a country of bicycles. Not that the Netherlander is always one of the favourites in the Tour de France – he loses too much time in the mountains for that. But the country does have the most bicycles per head of population in the world – one bicycle for each inhabitant. Many Netherlanders own more than one – an 'ordinary' one for everyday use, and a 'best' one for cycle trips, a favourite form of relaxation which owes much of its popularity to the flatness of the Dutch countryside. Families enjoying a bike ride, such as here in Hollum on the island of **Ameland** (above left) **and Woudrichem in North Brabant** (below left) **are a familiar sight. In the absence of cycling-mad family members and household pets, a baker in Sloten in Friesland goes out on his delivery bike with his favourite teddy bear** (below right). **The modern tandem, like this one with two lovely ladies from the seaside resort of Westkapelle in Zeeland, is made for intimate cycling pleasure** (far left, below). **For those who prefer speed to intimacy, the M5 Low Racer is the ultimate – a super-fast reclining bicycle on which the Netherlander Bram Moens established a world one-hour distance record** (above right). **We have come a long way from the traditional, old-fashioned 'grandma's bicycle', a machine that is as Dutch as the clog, the windmill and the tulip, and which quite rightly takes a prominent place in the performances of the show band Crescendo** (far left, above).

Skating

When Jack Frost reigns and the land of water becomes a land of ice, the whole of the Netherlands gets its skates on! Practically everywhere where there is a stretch of water races and non-competitive 'tours' are organized, even on meadows which have been specially flooded. Young children are taken to the local lake where, holding the hand of their parents or hanging on to the back of a kitchen chair, they take the first faltering steps on a slippery path that perhaps will lead to a career in match skating. Elsewhere in the city, on the canals of Amsterdam, for example (second photo from bottom), people can also enjoy skating. Experienced skaters, however, prefer to seek the openness of lakes and canals and make long trips through the magical winter landscape – in the IJsselmeer town of Hindeloopen in Friesland (above), for example, or at Kinderdijk in South Holland (large photo), where an exhausted young boy gets a tow from his father (below left). 'Koek-en-zopie' (refreshment) stalls appear along the most popular routes, like this one in the harbour of the IJsselmeer town of Monnickendam (second photo from top) in North Holland. Body and soul can be refreshed with hot sausages, thick pea soup and chocolate. Many skaters take along some alcoholic refreshment. Friesian herb bitters are very popular – according to those in the know they are an outstanding defence against anything and everything, including the crackling cold.

Social life

The Netherlander is a creature of pleasure and has a highly developed social life. Many people belong to clubs and go out to relax in their spare time. The 'brown café', a type of bar that derives its name from the cosiness and sense of security associated with wooden panelling and furniture, is very popular. But even the brownest café, like the café Hemingway in Utrecht (middle), has a terrace, because as long as the weather allows, the Netherlander prefers to sit outside – beside the water in Giethoorn in Overijssel (above), for example, or until late in the evening on Leidseplein, one of the most popular entertainment centres in Amsterdam (below).

Relaxation

In the Netherlands, of course, the water is an important source of relaxation and pleasure. On warm summer days the population heads en masse for the coast. On the beautiful beaches it becomes apparant just how incredibly densely populated the Netherlands is, although in most places it is less busy than in the famous resorts of Scheveningen (above) and Zandvoort. The open waters of the many lakes and pools, an El Dorado for watersports en-thusiasts, offer more peace and quiet. Seasoned sailors prefer the IJsselmeer (below) and the Friesian lakes. On beautiful days those Netherlanders who do not like water or crowds (and there are plenty of them) head in the opposite direction – into town or out into the countryside. The miniature city of Madurodam (middle) in The Hague, where children become giants, is a popular destination (see also page 56-57).

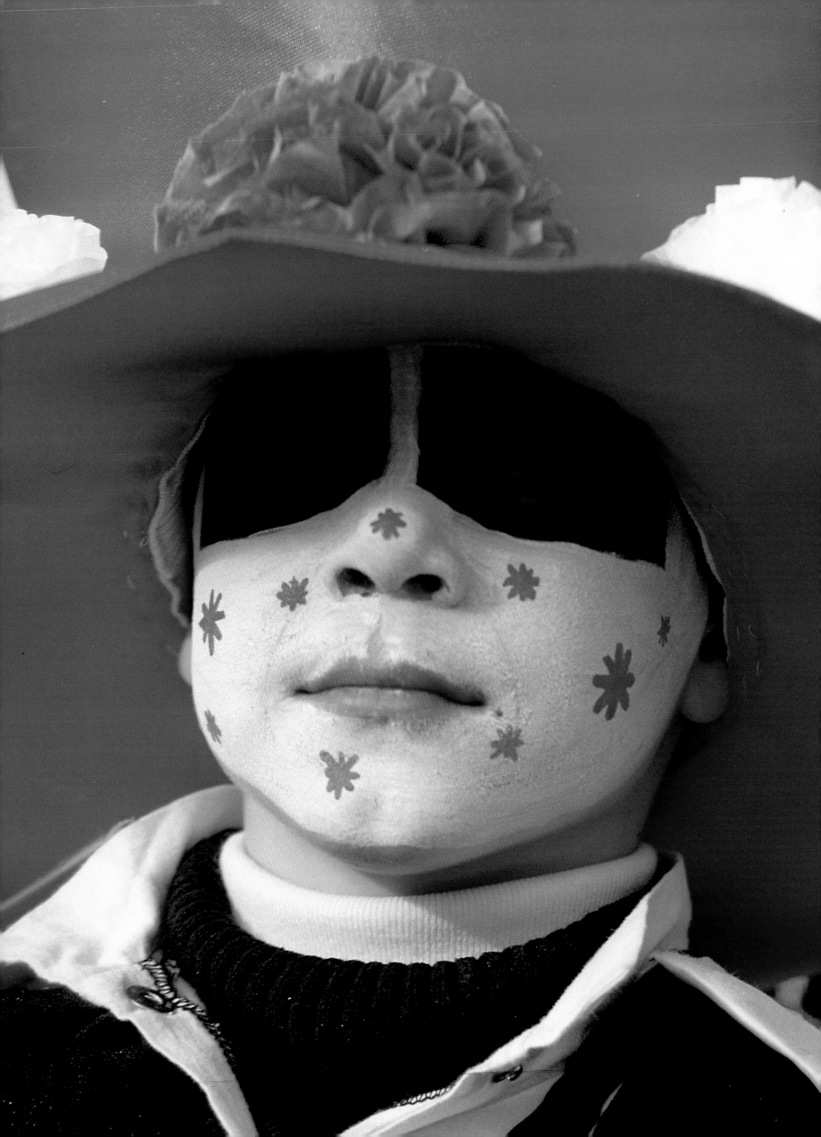

Festivities

N etherlanders are said to be rather sober. This is true to a large extent, but not altogether, for on certain occasions they really let their hair down. 'Koninginnedag' (the Queen's Birthday), carnival and big sporting events all have their own particular brand of 'oranjegekte' (orange madness). Other festivities, such as the typically Dutch family celebration of Sint-Nicolaas (Sinterklaas), that remarkable Turkish saint from Spain who speaks such excellent Dutch, are more modest.

Celebrations within the domestic circle

Broadly speaking, the Netherlander recognizes two types of festivity; those celebrated within his intimate circle and those of a public nature. To the first category belong the Christian celebrations of Easter, Whitsuntide and Christmas, as well as Sinterklaas (5 December), New Year's Eve and New Year's Day. The theme of these festivals is domestic conviviality. They are usually celebrated with family or friends and an extensive festive meal is often served. Birthdays follow much the same pattern. The person celebrating his birthday traditionally treats his guests to coffee and pastries, perhaps a meal, and in turn receives flowers and gifts. The fiftieth birthday is regarded as a milestone which justifies much more extensive celebrations. Often the person is lured by his family and friends to a restaurant or a café, where he is treated like royalty the whole evening.

To some extent marriages and wedding anniversaries can be compared with birthdays, except they are generally celebrated outside the home. Before a marriage, family and friends

The Queen's Birthday

Queen Beatrix visiting Marken, North Holland, on 'Koninginnedag', her official birthday and one of the most important festive days in the Netherlands (above). Queen Beatrix actually celebrates her birthday on 31 January, but seeing that the winter is not really suitable for a national party, when she ascended the throne in 1980 it was decided to stick to her mother's birthday – 30 April. On her birthday the Queen traditionally visits two districts, which spare neither cost nor effort to present their best face to 'Bea' and to receive her royally. In Marken two children, wearing the orange local costume (which is only worn on this day), perform a dance (right) and even the sheep are in their best party clothes (below)!

Page 92-93
Unrecognizably disguised during the Maastricht carnival in Limburg.
Small photo: **the Dutch tricolour.**

often organize a party to celebrate the last 'free' evening of the future bride and groom. Usually they are treated by their respective friends to a 'pub crawl'. Joking and jesting, witty gifts and a great deal of drinking are the order of the day. Instances where the bridegroom was delivered to the Registry Office on his wedding day as drunk as a lord and dressed in a gorilla costume have been known – the reason why many stag nights and hen parties take place well before the wedding day!

Public 'oranjegekte'

The Netherlander has a somewhat ambivalent attitude towards such celebrations, combining as they do the pleasure of a day off with the obligation of a family visit. Many are concerned about the 'party month' of December, in particular. Every year newspapers and magazines devote attention to the problem.

Family ties are noticeably less binding during the second type of celebration, the public festivities. First and foremost these festivities are opportunities for the sober Netherlander to really let off steam. Liberation Day (5 May) and carnival belong to this category, but the celebration of the Queen's Birthday (30 April) beats everything! In many places there are big 'free' flea markets (an excuse to clear out the attic!), street performers and sometimes fairground attractions. Throngs of people, in true party mood, shuffle from one attraction to the next. Orange, the colour of the Royal House, dominates. In the big cities, in particular, the day comes to its conclusion in lively chaos and ends with a thunderous fireworks display. Although the Netherlander is not a fervent monarchist, he would not miss this chance of a national festival for the world. The festivities on the occasion of Liberation Day (5 May) – the commemoration of the end of the German occupation during the Second World War – are somewhat similar, but officially this is celebrated only once every five years. On the evening before Liberation Day – 'Dodenherdenking' (the Commemoration of the Dead) – the whole country comes to a standstill as the dead of the Second World War are remembered.

Two types of carnival

Carnival, the four-day festival of ridicule, role reversal and dressing-up that precedes Lent, is largely celebrated in the predominantly Catholic southern provinces, particularly in North Brabant and Limburg. Elsewhere, many people shrug their shoulders at what they regard as 'vulgar' amusement, although there are carnival societies all over the country.

Besides traditional carnival there is also a 'tropical summer carnival', based on the South American model, and celebrated in Rotterdam on the last Saturday in July. Originally this was a festival celebrated by Antillians living in the Netherlands, but it has now grown into a magnificent multicul-

Above and below
Merriment and surprise battle for supremacy in these three young carnival celebrators who think they have recognized the long-dead painter Vincent van Gogh in the traditional parade.

Page 97
The celebration of the Queen's Birthday in Marken (see previous pages) **passes off peacefully and properly, according to protocol, but in the big cities it degenerates into happy chaos. People en masse take over the water on Prinsengracht in Amsterdam. Houseboats are boarded and a tourist 'round-trip' boat, surrounded by an armada of barely seaworthy craft, is threatened with shipwreck! Woe to the foreigner who wants to make a quick round trip before catching his plane!**

tural festival. Swinging to the sounds of merengue, tumba, calypso, salsa, samba and reggae, the fantastically-costumed procession weaves its way slowly through the city.

'Elfsteden' fever

It is not only on the Queen's Birthday, Liberation Day and during carnival that the Netherlander gives free rein to his emotions. He is also seized by 'oranjegekte' during important sports events. The successes of the national football team and the club teams Feyenoord, PSV and Ajax – since the days of the legendary Johan Cruijff the most popular and successful football club in the country – invariably result in spontaneous popular celebrations.

Nothing, however, can be compared to the fever that sweeps through the Netherlands in bitter winter weather. Then the whole country talks about nothing else but the possibility of an 'Elfstedentocht', a marathon skating event through eleven towns in Friesland. The media are obsessed by a single question: will the 'Tocht der Tochten' (Trek of Treks) take place? On every television channel meteorologists discuss such topics as the relationship between the thickness of the ice and wind speed, and the volunteer officials who supervise the quality of the ice along the course become national celebrities overnight. If eventually the go-ahead is given, a million Netherlanders, garlanded with musical instruments, wearing orange woolly caps and waving orange flags, converge on Friesland to cheer on and support the many thousands who are actually taking part. This is not an unnecessary luxury, because many of the participants are ill-prepared for the bitter cold, or lose their way in the darkness of the early morning or late evening. The joviality along the route is unprecedented. The Elfstedentocht is a true festival of fraternization.

Sinterklaas

Nevertheless, most Netherlanders when asked what the most popular Dutch festival is would not say the Elfstedentocht, but the festival of Sint-Nicolaas – Sinterklaas. This is celebrated on the evening of 5 December, the eve of the anniversary of the saint's death, when gifts are distributed in the saint's name in the family circle. 'Sinterklaasavond' is above all a festival for children, who, even though most of them know better, stubbornly insist that these gifts are not from their parents, but from the genial Saint himself.

There is no satisfactory answer to the question as to how this Byzantine saint has been transformed into the friend of Dutch children. The tradition is that he lived from 270 to 343 AD in the Turkish city of Myra, where he was bishop and performer of miracles. He owes his fame as the bringer of gifts to children to some of these miracles. Children were not his only concern, however – he was also the patron saint of sailors, traders, bankers, bakers, butchers, prostitutes, thieves and prisoners.

The Sint's reputation also appealed to the people's imagination in Europe and for a long time in the late Middle Ages he was the most popular saint in that part of the world. In 1087 Italian merchants even abducted his bones, which since then have rested in Bari. During the Reformation the 'Nicolaas cult' lost its significance. Nevertheless, he retained his popularity in the Calvinist Netherlands, probably because he had already become part of Dutch family life. The reason for this lay not only in his role of children's friend, but also in his moral significance. The Sint decided whether the children had been well-behaved, and depending on this judgement he rewarded or punished them. Naughty children were threatened with a beating or being carried off 'in Sinterklaas' sack'. Punishment was to be meted out by the Sint's trusty companion 'Zwarte Piet' (Black Peter) – the similarity of his role with the traditional role of the devil is difficult to ignore.

Because of this moral aspect the Sinterklaas festival is also popular among adults. They use all their imagination and ingenuity in preparing beautifully wrapped 'surprises' and writing poems to attach to them. Both gifts and poems are intended to 'reward' or 'punish' the recipients' good or bad points and give people an opportunity to pull each other's legs in a manner which would be unthinkable in everyday life. And having relieved their feelings in this way, they return to normal, everyday life, just as they do after exuberantly celebrating the Queen's Birthday or an important victory on the football field.

Football madness

Big chief 'Orange Feather' beats the drum in celebration after the Dutch football team has beaten neighbouring Belgium in the classic derby of the Low Countries (large photo). This 'Indian' is well-known in the stadiums and a living example of the joyful madness which takes over many Netherlanders at important football matches. This 'orange ostentation' is an emotional release with a highly playful undertone. Crazy attire is the rule rather than the exception (small photos). Since the days of the 'Black Tulip' Ruud Gullit, there is even a market for orange rasta hair-dos! The favourite battle song of the Dutch team – which plays in the colours of the royal house and is therefore known as 'Oranje' – is 'He has won, the silver fleet'. It is a reminder of a great feat of arms in the Netherlands' maritime history, the capture of the Spanish silver fleet. This fleet, laden with treasure, sailed every year from the Spanish possessions in America to Spain. In 1628 it was intercepted off Cuba by Admiral Piet Hein.

Carnival

Carnival in Maastricht. Impressive costumes are a feature of the celebration of this exuberant Catholic festival which precedes Lent. It mainly takes place in the 'Netherlands to the south of the great rivers', particularly in the provinces of Limburg and North Brabant. The great rivers form the border between the predominantly Catholic south and the largely Protestant north, where people often regard carnival as a rather vulgar entertainment. Nothing of the sort, retort seasoned carnival celebrators, who are of the opinion that the northerners base their ideas on the strange doings of their own isolated Carnival Associations and have not got a clue about what 'real' carnival is all about. The essence of carnival is forgetting normal, serious, everyday matters – or better still, turning them on their head. Dressing up and exuberant partying are part of it, of course, but certainly not vulgarity or coarse behaviour! But the southerners could not care less if northerners understand or not – as long as at the end of February they themselves can party in Maastricht, Den Bosch, Breda or Bergen op Zoom, where the festivities often go on long after the official four days are over.

The 'Elfstedentocht'

Almost every bitterly cold winter has one day when at five o'clock in the morning more than two million excited Netherlanders sit down in front of their televisions. At the same time a million of their compatriots slither and slide in complete darkness over the frozen ditches and canals of Friesland, decked out with banners, flags and musical instruments, their faces smeared with fat as protection against the bitter cold. It seems that the Netherlands has taken leave of its senses. And indeed it has, because in Leeuwarden the Elfstedentocht – a 200-kilometre-long skating marathon through eleven towns in Friesland, starting and finishing in the Friesian capital – is about to begin! This marathon is only organized in very cold winters – from 1909 to 1997 the event took place only fifteen times – and creates an excitement that has no parallel. Those taking part – more than 16,000 – are received as heroes in the towns (above) and driven along by the cheering throngs and the noise of countless 'oompa' bands, including the police brass band (below). A sea of orange awaits the first arrivals at the finish (second photo from top). The 'Tocht der Tochten' (Trek of Treks) is the National Festival of National Festivals. Apart from the elite racers (second photo from bottom), the participants (large photo) adhere to the Olympic ideal – taking part is more important than winning. And a good thing, too, because thousands fail to complete the course, felled by exhaustion and the combination of bitter cold and strong winds which can easily send the temperature plummeting to twenty below zero. It also makes a contribution to the Dutch language with concepts such as 'klunen' (running across wooden sections to avoid a patch of poor ice or to change from one canal to another), and 'windwak' (where the wind disturbs the surface of the water and stops it freezing). Such sections require an 'ijs-transplantatie' (large blocks of ice are manouvered into place and sprayed with water so they bind together).

Sint-Nicolaas – Sinterklaas

At the beginning of December the Netherlands falls under the spell of the festival of Sint-Nicolaas, which reaches its climax on 'pakjesavond' (parcels evening) on 5 December. A few weeks earlier, children throng to the waterside to greet the jovial bishop, who traditionally arrives from Spain on a steamboat. No child stops to wonder how the Sint manages to arrive at more than one place at the same time – here he is arriving in 's-Graveland in North Holland (page 105). Nor do they wonder whether his ramshackle 'tub' is really suitable for a long voyage from Spain, or why the Byzantine bishop comes from Spain instead of Turkey, his fatherland. The Sint's association with Spain dates from the Middle Ages, when that exotic country was regarded as the cradle of all that was beautiful and pleasant. Moreover, it was teeming with Moors, the model for the Sint's faithful helper, Zwarte Piet (Black Peter). Piet personifies the devil (black with the soot of hell) and people believed the Sint had forced him to become his servant. Even today, he represents the sterner side of Sint-Nicolaas. On 5 December the Sint asks the children whether they have been well-behaved or not (above) – good children receive presents, Piet threatens naughty children with a beating or tells them he will take them back to Spain in his sack. While traditionally the Sint travels the country on a grey horse, modern-day Piets use bicycles (below), emphasizing the thoroughly Dutch nature of the Sinterklaas festival!

Moroccan girls, dressed in traditional festive clothing and their hands painted with henna on the occasion of a wedding. In addition to more than 160,000 Turks and a number of smaller groups from other Mediterranean countries, some 120,000 Moroccans live in the Netherlands.

Above
A float bearing the 'Golden Coach' made of flowers, at the South Holland seaside resort of Noordwijk in the traditional Bollenstreek floral procession. At the end of April every year a procession of floats leaves Haarlem and travels to Noordwijk via Lisse. The floats carry lavish creations made from more than one and a half million hyacinths, 25 thousand tulips and 25 thousand narcissus. The real Golden Coach is the traditional means of transport in which the reigning monarch rides to the Binnenhof in The Hague on the third Tuesday in September (Prince's Day) for the ceremonial opening of the new parliamentary year.

Middle
Adorned in a king-size hat displaying the city's coat of arms, an Amsterdammer takes part in the revelry of the Queen's birthday.

Below
Participants in the annual Gay Day parade through the centre of Amsterdam. The festive manifestation of the homosexual movement emphasizes the liberal climate of the Netherlands in general and that of the capital in particular.

Above
A dance group performing during the Pasar Malam Besar (Great Evening Market), a ten-day event held every year in June at the Malieveld in The Hague. This festival is the largest Indo-European festival in Europe and a very important event for the large community which has links with the former colony of the Dutch East Indies, present-day Indonesia. After the declaration of Indo-nesian independence 80,000 Netherlanders, 180,000 people of mixed Dutch-Indone-sian blood (Indos) and 12,500 Moluccans came to the Netherlands. Many of them settled in The Hague.

Middle
The Gay Parade passes along the canals of Amsterdam.

Below
The Antillian 'Little Miss' election during the annual Kwakoe festival in Amsterdam. This festival has grown from a football competition between Surinam teams into a huge manifestation which attracts hundreds of thousands of people. Surinamers form one of the biggest ethnic groups in the Netherlands. Round the time of the proclamation of Surinam independence in 1975 about 145,000 people, one third of the country's population, emigrated to the Netherlands. The present Suri-nam community consists of more than 200,000 people and is itself a mosaic of ethnic groups. The biggest of these are the Creoles (descendants of African slaves transported to Surinam by the Dutch), Hindustanis and Javanese (descendants of contract labourers from the British East Indies and Java respectively). There are about 80,000 Antillians in the Netherlands.

The economy

The Netherlands is traditionally a nation of transporters and traders. Because of its geographical position on the North Sea and at the mouths of three great European rivers it forms, as it were, a natural transit port. In the 17th century trade brought the Netherlands unprecedented prosperity. Although the economic balance has changed fundamentally since then, the position of the Netherlands in the top 10 richest countries, together with that of Rotterdam as the biggest port in the world, shows that it is still a thriving country.

From fisherman to merchant

It was fish, not trade, that first tempted the Netherlander to put to sea. But once he set sail he discovered there was a lot more to harvest than what he hauled up in his nets. He learned to regard the sea as a highway which offered lucrative opportunities in transport and trade. In the late Middle Ages the Netherlander gradually became the cargo carrier of Europe, and later of the world. He engaged in a flourishing trade with the Baltic countries, Southern Europe, Africa, the Far East and America. A graphic illustration of the Netherlands' powerful maritime status is that of all the ships which passed the Öresund between 1560 and 1650 more than sixty percent flew the Dutch flag. In around 1700 more than eight hundred ships sailed every year for the Baltic countries from the Holland and Zeeland provinces alone. Dutch ships carried an unprecedented variety of products. From the Baltic countries, and Norway and Sweden came grain, wood, hemp, stockfish and iron; from France, Spain and Portugal salt, wine, leather and wool; from Crete muscatel and raisins; from Smyrna car-

Page 110-111
The Eemsmond wind park towers above the North Groningen landscape. With its 134 wind turbines, Eemsmond is the biggest wind park in Europe and supplies sufficient energy to provide some 25,000 households with electricity. In the background is the windmill 'Goliath', built in 1897 to maintain the water level in the Eemspolder.
Small photo: **drawn up in battle order, Edam cheeses wait for buyers. The North Holland town of Edam has enjoyed a great reputation as a cheese producer since the end of the 16th century. Eighty million cheeses are produced each year, most of them destined for export. An Edam cheese is made in a bowl-shaped form, known as a 'kaaskop' (cheese head), a word the Belgians mockingly use to describe a Netherlander. Cheeses intended for export are given a red paraffin coating to help conserve them.**

Above and below
The Netherlands has a name to uphold as a producer of meat and dairy products. Cattle markets, where farmers and dealers meet to do business, are held all over the country.

pets; from Persia silk; from Surinam sugar and coffee; from the East Indies spices, silk, indigo, cloth, carpets, diamonds, rubies, pearls, ebony, and porcelain. Fishing and whaling remained almost as important. In April 1690 alone more than two hundred ships set sail for Greenland, where some 1400 whales were caught.

The Golden Age

Trade brought unprecedented prosperity. In the 17th century the Netherlands was the richest country in Northern Europe. Amsterdam grew into the trading centre of the world and along the canals rose the stately merchants' houses which still determine the monumental nature of the inner city. It is to this period that the Netherlands owes its reputation as a great maritime power, a reputation which in the 19th and 20th centuries was given a new impulse by the powerful hydraulic engineering projects carried out in the Low Countries. This reputation partly rested on the activities – not always benign – of two renowned trading companies; the Dutch East India Company (VOC), founded in 1602 as a merger between companies in Amsterdam, Enkhuizen, Hoorn, Rotterdam, Delft and Middelburg, and the West India Company (WIC), founded in 1621. The VOC operated largely in Asia, the WIC in America and, largely in the context of the flourishing slave trade, West Africa. The VOC in particular was successful for a long period – for more than a century and a half this multinational was the greatest enterprise in the world. One of the WIC's outstanding exploits was the setting up of the trading post of Nieuw-Amsterdam, which the governor Peter Stuyvesant handed over to Britain in 1664, and which has since been known as New York.

Besides being a trading nation, the Netherlands in those days was a formidable sea power, which was not averse to taking violent action when freedom of trade was endangered. Three trade wars were fought with protectionist Britain. Just like the military exploits of famous admirals such as De Ruyter and Tromp, the colonial adventures of the Netherlands were also in the context of trade. It was not imperialistic but commercial motives that were at the root of the lengthy domination of the Dutch East Indies (today's Indonesia), Surinam and the Dutch Antilles. But the Golden Age was not exclusively an age of traders and maritime heroes. Prosperity was the basis of an impressive cultural flowering. Painting, in particular, flourished, as can be seen in the Amsterdam Rijksmuseum's wonderful collection. Among the hundreds of Dutch masters are world famous painters such as Rembrandt van Rijn, Frans Hals, Johannes Vermeer and Jan Steen, who found life much tougher when they were alive than their posthumous fame might suggest. Vermeer's work even hung on his baker's wall as security for a debt of 617 guilders.

Late industrialization

Economic growth stagnated in the 18th century, one reason being that more countries were transporting their own goods. For the Netherlanders, who largely traded in foreign goods and who did not have any meaningful domestic industries of their own, this was a heavy blow. What domestic industry there was was concentrated in the ports and mainly involved processing imported products which were then transhipped to other countries. This imbalance meant that at the beginning of the 19th century the Netherlands was outstripped by her arch-rival England, the cradle of the Industrial Revolution.

Countries such as Germany and Belgium were also industrialized before the Netherlands, where this process only began at the end of the 19th century. Partly because of the deep economic crisis of the thirties it would take until after the Second World War before the Netherlands once again ranked as one of the world's richest countries. The country experienced huge economic growth, following in the footsteps of Germany. This is shown, among other things, by the expansion of wholly or partly owned Dutch multinationals such as Philips, Unilever and Shell, companies which brought world-wide recognition to the Netherlands. Another important consequence of the German renaissance was that, as a port, Amsterdam was eclipsed by Rotterdam. Strategically situated Rotterdam is the biggest port in the world and has an important transhipment function for the European Union.

Dutch industry specializes in high-quality products, but because of the scarcity of raw materials – other than natural gas, which makes an important contribution to the national treasury – it is highly dependent on other countries. For this reason a number of important industries, particularly the petrochemical and iron and steel industries, are situated on, or near, the coast. Another feature is that because of the limited domestic market the big industrial concerns are very internationally oriented. The Netherlands is the headquarters of a strikingly large number of multinational enterprises, proving once again that industry is closely linked to distribution and transport.

The Flying Dutchman

The face of the Dutch economy abroad is not only determined by companies such as Philips, but also by agricultural products, ranging from bulbs to pedigree Friesian cattle. Cheese, butter, powdered milk and beer, products which the Netherlands exports more of than any other country, are important, too. Other foodstuffs are also exported in large quantities. This is partly due to the high productivity of Dutch agriculture, which is ultramodern, large-scale, capital-intensive and labour-extensive. Less than three percent of Netherlanders earn their living in the agriculture sector as opposed to more than fifty percent in 1900. Horticultural productivity is also high. Hothouse cultivation has increased enormously and for many foreigners the imposing 'glass

Above
Cargo boat on the Waal at Nijmegen in Gelderland. Although inland navigation has long been superseded by road transport, it is still of great importance in water-rich Netherlands.

Above left
Fishing boats in Colijnsplaat on the Oosterschelde. The centuries-old Dutch fishing industry has suffered severely from over-fishing in the North Sea and the imposition of international limitations on catches.

Below left
A miller at work in the paint mill De Kat in the Zaanse Schans in North Holland. The mill assumed its present form in 1959 when two mills dating from around 1780 were combined into one. Among other things, De Kat produces antique paint pigments. It is the last of the 55 paint mills which once stood along the river Zaan, and probably the last paint mill in the world.

Below
A windmill in the Schermer-polder in North Holland.

Right
A Shell refinery in Pernis. The development of Pernis illustrates the enormous expansion of the port of Rotterdam. When Shell built the first refinery here in 1936, Pernis was still a long way from the city. Now the port area stretches far beyond Pernis, which is the centre for processing crude oil. The 'black gold' is delivered at eight petroleum docks by gigantic oil tankers and processed into petroleum products.

Above and below
Details of the industrial complex of Air Products Pernis, producer of industrial gas.

city' in the Westland is just as familiar an image as the airport at Schiphol or the port of Rotterdam, the transit points which are so important for the export of Dutch specialities.

The strong growth of these 'mainports' illustrates that trade, transport, distribution and the service industries remain of inestimable importance to the Dutch economy. Schiphol, for years one of the world's best airports, plays an important role in both passenger and cargo transport and is the home base of the world's oldest airline, 'Flying Dutchman' KLM.

Just as in the 17th century, the tiny Netherlands is a trade centre with great allure, particularly as far as high-quality products are concerned. It is significant that more than forty percent of all European distribution centres are established in the Netherlands. It is no wonder that the accessibility of foreign markets and the lifting of trade barriers are still themes which concern the Netherlander more than most people. It is for this reason the Netherlands has always been a firm supporter of European integration. Although the days when the Netherlands drummed up her admirals to enforce freedom of trade are gone for good, sometimes the Netherlander is not all that far removed from his 17th-century merchant ancestors.

A vision from the 17th century – Zaanse Schans near Zaandijk in North Holland. With its seven windmills and traditional (ware)houses this little village is a reminder of the hey-day of the Zaanstreek, 'the oldest industrial region in the world'. The first sawmill was built in 1596 and was the start of what became an extensive and varied industrial area. A few decades later there were about six hundred mills in the region and by the 18th century there were more than a thousand. They sawed Norwegian and German timber, mixed paint pigments, polished marble, processed hemp, pressed oil, stamped tobacco, treated paper and lead, and ground foodstuffs such as cocoa, mustard and grain. The Zaanstreek was a rich industrial region. Its shipyards were world-renowned; in 1797 the Russian Tsar Peter the Great came to Zaandam to study shipbuilding. In the middle of the 19th century, however, the mills made way for factories which worked on steam power. This phase in Zaanse history will forever be linked with the founding of famous Dutch provisions companies such as Verkade, Honig, Duyvis and Albert Heijn. The mills and buildings in the Zaanse Schans are a reminder of the days when people here literally lived off the wind. They are all authentic, mostly from other places in the Zaanstreek and rebuilt here on the Schans. Although many are accessible to the general public, they are not museums. People live and – according to established Zaanse custom – work here.

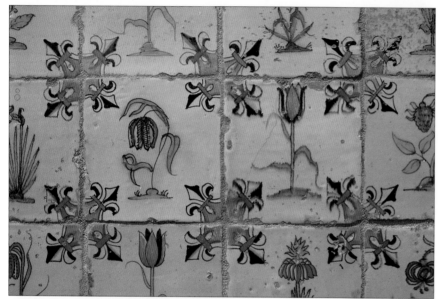

Flower Power

Nowhere is the saying 'your money's worth more at the market' more applicable than at the Dutch flower markets, of which Amsterdam is the best known, but Utrecht's the loveliest (below right). In a country where the cultivation of bulbs and flowers has been raised to an art form, flowers are cheaper and more generally available than anywhere else in the world. Bulbs have been cultivated in the Netherlands since the end of the 16th century. At that time the tulip – which quickly became a much-loved theme on Delft blue tiles (left, middle) – was the favourite. In 1636-1637 the lively bulb trade led to extravagant speculation and many a citizen lost all he possessed. The centre of today's trade in cut flowers and pot plants is the Aalsmeer flower auction in North Holland, the biggest flower auction – and also the biggest industrial building – in the world (above left and above right). Seventeen million flowers and two million pot plants change hands here every day. Roses (two hundred varieties) are by far the favourite. More than eighty percent of the flowers sold goes abroad. Ornamental plant cultivation largely takes place in hot-houses, in contrast to bulb cultivation which covers an area of about 120,000 hectares. The most cultivated bulbs are the tulip, hyacinth, gladiola, narcissus and lily and these, too, are exported to the four corners of the world. The most important bulb-growing regions are the Kop (Head) of North Holland and the area between Haarlem and Leiden, with centres such as Lisse (below left) and Noordwijkerhout (right, middle). The Keukenhof, the largest flower garden in the world and an important tourist attraction (middle), is near Lisse.

Agriculture

Although a large part of the
Netherlands is utilized for agriculture, very few Netherlanders
(less than three percent)
actually earn their living from
the land. The farming industry
is large-scale and ultramodern.
The farms seem like islands in
a sea of fields and meadows
(small photo). In many activities,
such as bringing in the harvest
in the hills of South Limburg
(above), nowadays there is
hardly a human being in sight.
Modernization of agriculture
has led to a great increase in
production and there are few
countries where the yield per
hectare is greater than in the
Netherlands. Hothouse cultivation in the Westland (middle) is
a good example of modern
management. Vegetables,
fruit and flowers, mainly for
export, are grown in the 'glass

city' around Naaldwijk in South
Holland. The famous Dutch
dairy industry, which is also
strongly export-oriented, is
ultramodern, too. The days
when the cows were milked by
hand have long gone and the
cheese market in Edam (below)
is now only part of folklore.

Cattle breeding

The cattle breeding sector is just as modern, though some traditions – for example, the haggling between farmer and dealer at the cattle market in Purmerend in North Holland (above) – might suggest otherwise! Breeders strive for a continual improvement in the quality of the cattle using the most modern breeding methods. Cattle breeding is an extremely serious industry and, furthermore, big business. A champion breeding bull, such as Sunny Boy, a legend in his own lifetime, whose sperm is good for an insemination every three minutes and exported to dozens of countries, brings enormous amounts of money to the coffers. The Dutch cow (middle) has had a good reputation for centuries. The Friesian pedigree cow is world famous, and for a long time gave the Friesian farmer an apparently unassailable position in cattle breeding and the export of dairy products. There was a great deal of laughter when in other provinces and elsewhere in the world types of cattle were bred which surpassed the Friesian cow in quality. The sheeted or belted cow is seldom seen in the meadows of the Netherlands. This ancient Dutch breed, recognizable by its white 'sheet' or 'belt', yields little milk and is therefore seldom kept. In fact, this animal almost became extinct. In the framework of the conservation of nature – and as a hobby – the belted cow is again being bred on a small scale – in Lexmond in Utrecht (below), among other places – and many farmers now have one or two in their meadows.

The Golden Age

The 17th century – or to be more exact the period between about 1585 and 1670 – has gone down in history as the 'Golden Age'. It was a time in which the Netherlands experienced enormous economic expansion and Amsterdam grew into a global trading centre. It was during this period that many of the characteristic canal houses in the capital (middle, below) were built by immensely wealthy merchants. Although the prosperity was partly due to the flourishing fishing industry, processing industries and agriculture, it was the achievements of the merchant trading fleet, in particular those of the Dutch East India Company (voc), which most appeal to the imagination. This enterprise, founded in 1602, was the first multinational company in the world and for more than one and a half centuries it dominated trade in East Asia. Chinese porcelain imported by the voc was the source of inspiration for the Delft pottery industry, which applied itself to Asian imitations as well as to typical Dutch products (above left and below left). Delft Blue was known throughout Europe. It is still manufactured by traditional methods by – among others – De Porceleyne Fles concern, which was founded in 1653 (left, middle). The ships of the voc – to our eyes hardly more than cockleshells – decorate many a facade, including this 17th-century warehouse in Hoorn (below right). A replica of the voc ship De Amsterdam can be seen in Amsterdam (above right). The gold of the Golden Age formed the basis for a great cultural flourishing, which expressed itself in painting, in particular. Perhaps the true symbol of this is Rembrandt's masterpiece De Nachtwacht, a 'schuttersstuk' (a painting of civilian militia), dating from 1642 (middle, above). It is one of the high points of the collection of the Amsterdam Rijksmuseum.

Above left
A hot-rolling strip mill in the Koninklijke Hoogovens (Royal Blast Furnaces) in IJmuiden in North Holland. Hot-rolled steel is used all over the world in the building, car and packaging industries.

Below left
Fast-growing Schiphol, to the south-west of Amsterdam, is one of the best airports in the world. Schiphol plays an important role in the international transport of passengers and freight and is the home base of the national airline company, KLM, the world's oldest airline.

Above right
Messages from the past are recorded by the twelve huge dishes of West Europe's largest radio telescope, near Westerbork in Drenthe. Because the skies above the Netherlands are not clear enough to allow the cosmos to be studied through an 'ordinary' telescope, this is done by 'catching' sounds. Among other things, this telescope receives signals from the period in which the universe was being formed, billions of light years ago.

Below right
The World Trade Center in Rotterdam, built in 1987 to the design of Groosman and Partners and known by the public as the 'cigarette lighter'. On the left is a detail of the Beurs (Stock Exchange), one of the few buildings in the centre of Rotterdam which survived the German bombardment in May 1940.

A proud port

The port of Rotterdam is the largest in the world. Approximately three hundred million tons of goods are handled here every year. About eighty percent of this is intended for transhipment, most of it abroad. The port owes its important 'hub' function to its excellent links to the North Sea and with the European hinterland, as well as to its good road and rail links and the proximity of Rotterdam Airport and Schiphol. Crude oil accounts for about a third of shipments. This is discharged in eight petroleum docks (large photo) and processed in huge refineries within the harbour area. The petrochemical industries are in the immediate vicinity – Rotterdam is also an important industrial centre.

The completion of the eighteen-kilometre-long Nieuwe Waterweg in 1872 was a great step in Rotterdam's development into a port of world-wide importance. At the same time, a start was made on the development of the south bank of the Maas. One building here was the proud head office of the Holland-America Line, now the Hotel New York (second photo from bottom). After this, the port also grew in a westerly direction. In 1931 the Waalhaven was completed, at that time the biggest dock in the world.

Further expansion followed immediately after the Second World War – the Botlek, Europoort – a name which indicated that Rotterdam now regarded itself as being the 'Poort naar Europa' (Gateway to Europe) – and the Maasvlakte, where an ultramodern container port was built (above and below). Nowadays the port area stretches along the entire length of the Nieuwe Waterweg and has even extended into the sea. Since 1963 the port is not just the Gateway to Europe, but also the largest in the world – the pride of Rotterdam.

Photographer & writer

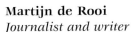

Frans Lemmens
Photographer

Frans Lemmens (1953) – seen in the photo with his partner and assistant Marjolijn van Steeden – is one of the Netherlands most prominent photographers.

Lemmens, born and bred in Schimmert (Limburg), is a true globetrotter. After completing his studies at the Netherlands School of Business Nijenrode, the world became his studio. He worked for years in Africa as a development-aid worker, travelled all the continents as a tour guide, and then returned to Africa as controller of food aid. He developed his photographic talent during this period of his life.

In 1986 Lemmens became a freelance documentary photographer. In this capacity he undertook a number of unique expeditions. He crossed the Sahara on foot with a party of Tuaregs and their camel caravan, accompanied the Chilean navy to Antarctica and flew around the world in a Catalina flying boat.

Lemmens made his international breakthrough in 1989 with his magnificent book 'Algerian Sahara'. At the moment he is under contract to The Image Bank, the largest photo agency in the world, and publishes his work in dozens of authoritative magazines and professional journals both in the Netherlands and abroad. Since 1993 the Netherlands has been an important theme in Lemmens' oeuvre. The familiarity, originality and high aesthetic content of his Holland photos, which appear in the form of reports, calendars and postcards, compel wide admiration. 'Visions of the Netherlands' is the undisputed crown on this element of his work. All Lemmens' favourite themes – nature, landscape, culture, architecture and tourism – are amply portrayed in this book.

Martijn de Rooi
Journalist and writer

Martijn de Rooi (Amsterdam, 1956) graduated with distinction as a sociologist from Utrecht University. Until 1988 he was associated with this university as a researcher. Since then he has worked as a freelance (travel) journalist and editor for various magazines and publishers and as a writer for a wide variety of clients. Together with Frans Lemmens, he has made reports in the Netherlands and abroad, including one on life in the oases of the Sahara. He has also written travel guides to Egypt, Indonesia and Cyprus. As an editor, he has worked for years for the leading publisher Periplus Editions, based in Singapore, whose publications include the Indonesia Adventure Guides and a large number of standard works in the field of Asiatic art and culture.

Since the start of his career Lemmens has worked with professional Nikon equipment. As a photographer who often works in extremely remote locations and under exceptionally difficult circumstances, absolute confidence in the tools of his trade is of the greatest importance. His standard equipment consists of three F 90-X bodies, three zoom lenses (20-35 mm, 35-70 mm and 80-200 mm), a telephoto lens (300 mm), a macro lens (60 mm), a fisheye lens (16 mm), a perspective control lens (28 mm) and two SB-26 flashes. To allow greater creativity, all the bodies are fitted with an MF-26 multi-control back.

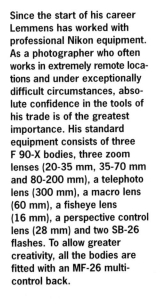